I

Praise for *Don't Just Give It Away ...*

"Every once in a while a book comes along which, though written with down-to-earth clarity and simplicity, carries within its covers a clarion call to reverse the flow of power and unsettle the status quo in an entire facet of society. This is that book."

> – Stephen C. Nill, J.D., Editor
> *American Philanthropy*
> *Review/CharityChannel.com*

"Mrs. Rafferty's experience and perspective are beautifully presented using commonsense language and practical tips."

> – Virginia Esposito, President
> *National Center for*
> *Family Philanthropy*

"Indispensable and iconoclastic...Don't Just Give It Away gores the 'sacred cows' of charity and philanthropy as we traditionally think of them."

> – Peter B. Manzo, J.D.,
> Executive Director
> *Center for Nonprofit Management*
> *of Southern California*

"Don't Just Give It Away celebrates the joy of giving while bringing perspective and light to a subject that needed to be demystified."

> – William P. Massey, President
> *National Charities Information*
> *Bureau*

"(It) forced me to examine my own beliefs about the role I play in society."

"Thoroughly engaging...Don't Just Give It Away makes the philanthropic process a clear, simple, and meaningful one."

"Don't Just Give It Away makes it brilliantly clear: 'business as usual' shouldn't – and won't – cut it with funders anymore.

Smart Generosity

Everything You Need to Know About
Charity, Philanthopy and Giving Wisely

Renata J. Rafferty

WORD
PRESS

Seven Word Press
Indian Wells, California

This publication is designed to provide accurate and authoritative information on the subject of philanthropy. While all of the stories and anecdotes described in the book are based on true experience, many of the names are pseudonyms, and some situations have been changed slightly to protect each individual's privacy. It is sold with the understanding that neither the Author nor the Publisher is engaged in rendering legal, financial, or other professional advice or services by publishing this book. As each individual situation is unique, questions relevant to philanthropy and personal or institutional finance and specific to the individual or organization should be addressed to an appropriate professional to ensure that the situation has been evaluated carefully and appropriately. The Author and Publisher specifically disclaim any liability, loss or risk that is incurred as a consequence, directly or indirectly, of the use and application of any of the contents of this work.

The author is grateful for permission to reprint the Foreword written by Paul Newman that previously appeared in Don't Just Give It Away

Published by Seven Word Press, a division of Rafferty Consulting Group

Visit our Website at www.SevenWordPress.com

The Seven Word Press name and logo and the Smart Generosity name are trademarks of Rafferty Consulting Group Incorporated

Library of Congress Control Number: 2008909397

Rafferty, Renata J.
  Smart generosity: everything you need to know about charity, philanthropy and giving wisely / Renata J. Rafferty.
      p. cm.
  Includes index.
  ISBN 978-0-9821728-0-3

Cover and book designed by Tara Blessinger, Blessinger Design www.BlessingerDesign.com

Printed in the United States of America

For information about purchasing this book for business or promotional use, or for special sales and quantity discounts, please contact Seven Word Press:
            SpecialMarkets@SevenWordPress.com.

TABLE OF CONTENTS

‹ܐܐ›

Acknowledgements

A NEW URGENCY ...

IN THE YEARS SINCE THE 1999 PUBLICATION OF Don't Just Give It Away (on which this book is based), reform of the charitable sector took on a new urgency in my personal life. My dear husband and partner, Jerome Rafferty, was diagnosed with Lewy body dementia (LBD) – the second most prevalent form of dementia after Alzheimer's disease.

Despite the fact that up to 30% of all dementia patients may have Lewy body, you probably have never heard of it. Medical professionals are mostly unaware of it, and even neurology specialists frequently misdiagnose LBD. It is a disease that combines the worst aspects of Alzheimer's and Parkinson's, and is progressive, degenerative, incurable.

For the first time in my life, I found myself looking through the other end of the charity telescope, searching for help and information. I assumed that with my experience and knowledge of this sector I would be able to reach out and assemble a simple profile of available services and programs that would assure a continuum of medical, psychological and emotional care for my family during the course of this devastating illness.

I experienced a merry-go-round of calls, letters and visits and learned that collaboration, or just simple cooperation, between charities is still the exception. Competition, turf-protection, and isolationism among organizations is prevalent. I experienced, as a client, the woeful mismanagement of some of our nation's largest and best-known chapter-based charities.

I also experienced wonderful and even amazing service from some boots-on-the-ground organizations...some famous, like the Mayo Clinic, and some little-known, under-funded, and volunteer-based, such as the Lewy Body Dementia Association (www.lbda.org).

I believe the structure and management of our community organizations often compound the stress of people in need, and it's our families, as much as anyone, who pay the price.

What is the most efficient and effective way to raise all charities to their highest level of performance and service? Be smart with your donations. Expect – even demand – great things from the charities you support, and they will improve. Require accountability and transparency as conditions of your gifts, and nonprofits will respond.

No regulator, no public official, no oversight board, academic group, world-wide symposium or think-tank holds as much power and influence as you do, as we do, to mold the charitable sector and its constituent organizations into a force for the greater good...and for the simple good.

I pray that your family will never face the devastation – and desolation – of progressive dementia, especially Lewy body. And I pray that no family ever turns to the charitable sector in their time of greatest need or hope to encounter disappointment.

I share the content of this book with you as a gift of empowerment – power to transform our charities for the love – and highest service – of mankind.

MY DEEPEST APPRECIATION ...

There are many that I would like to thank for contributing to this book, to my sanity, and to our family spirit during the period that Smart Generosity was being completed.

On a daily basis, whether by e-mail, phone or personal visit, I could count on my fellow "tapiocans" to reach out with whatever Jerome or I needed, personally or professionally. Not by coincidence, these individuals are also among the most prominent consultants and practitioners in the philanthropic sector today. So, I thank my dearest friends and long-time colleagues: Hildy Gottlieb, Jeane Vogel, Mari Lane Gewecke, Nathan Garber, Dimitri Petropolis, Michael Wyland, Mark Riffey, Bill Krueger, Jane Garthson, Susan Smith, and Andrew Grant.

Stephen Nill has been my friend, my attorney, and my fellow crusader in the battle against charity fraud for more than a decade. Through Charity Channel.com, he has brought together tens of thousands of professionals in the nonprofit/NGO sector from across the globe for peer discussion, debate, and assistance on topics ranging from the law of exempt organizations, to development strategies. You are all invited to join in.

Three women who, collectively, have supported and encouraged me in every way possible during this time are Carol Kauffman, Doris Buffett, and Ruth Ann Harnisch. Bless all three of you!

Only fellow sojourners through "Lewyland" can appreciate the pain, frustration and exhaustion of slowly losing someone you love to this wretched disease. These smart, strong ladies have been my spirit guides through LBD, always there, especially in the middle of the night, to offer wisdom, advice, a tip or a joke: Marjorie Carmen, Irene Selak, Angela Taylor, Robin Riddle, and Dorthea Perrin. You, along with the Lewy Body Dementia Association and all of its forum participants, save me every day.

I would like to thank my colleagues in the wealth management world, especially Rob O'Dell of LVM Capital Management, who introduced me to the International Association of Advisors in Philanthropy. AIP is the professional organization of wealth managers and financial planners dedicated to sharing the beauty (and bounty) of philanthropy with their clients. Thank you to Randy Fox, Johnne Syverson, Bob Thompson, Jerry Nuerge, and Les Winston; and Drake Zimmerman, Yale Levey, Richard Krasney, and Sean Stannard-Stockton.

With deep affection, I thank Judy Vossler, Susan Francis, Marsha Friedman/EMSI and Beth Morrison, who were there to support me.

And to two special family members, thank you for simply being... Sarah Phelps, our daughter from another mother, and Monica Tay Belej.

Shawna and Dick Farmer, we could count on you to do anything (and did!). You are two of the most honorable people I know and it has been my privilege to fight the good fight with you.

To Patty and Arthur Newman, who suffered a deep, personal loss just days before this book went to press, thank you for facilitating your dear brother Paul's contribution to this book. It is my privilege to share his and Arthur's memories about the profound effect their parents had on the men they grew up to be.

Linda Kuczma and Nancy Cruise, you saved my spirits and my house many times over. Thank you for helping me with tons of "stuff" – literally and figuratively.

If you love the simple elegance of the look of this book, Tara Blessinger of Blessinger Design in Evansville, Indiana, deserves all of the credit. You are simply the best, and most accommodating, designer I've ever had the pleasure to work with. Thank you for your years of support and patience, and for your familiar greetings of "Hey, beautiful!" or "Hello, lovely!" which never failed to pick me up.

Three souls are always with me…my beloved Babcia, Klara Plawinska, my brilliant brother, Edward Daroszewski, and my courageous father, Chester Daroszewski. You all left this earth much too early, but your imprints on my soul and character manifest every single day.

And then there were three…my sister Barbara Bazell, whose mind and soul amaze me and whose joie de vivre inspires me, and my mother Irene Daroszewski, who is my role model for strength and perseverance. You have been my stalwarts, and I'm still overwhelmed by your willingness to uproot your own lives just to try and make ours a little easier.

But most of all, thank you, my dear Jerome, for your love, support, graciousness, good humor and trust, "four" sure and for eternity.

FOREWORD

by Paul Newman

I F SOMEONE ASKED ME WHETHER I WAS RAISED TO BE A "PHILANTHROPIST",
I'd probably have to say no. But as I look back and think about what messages I grew up with in my home, I'd have to say I was raised to think about the needs of the people around me.

My brother Arthur and I grew up in Shaker Heights, Ohio. My father and my Uncle Joe owned the largest sporting goods store in the state. What a great business for a kid's dad to be in! Unless, of course, it's 1929 and the country is entering the worst Depression of its history.

As you can imagine, trying to move sporting goods while people were desperately trying to keep food on the table was not an easy proposition. Other men might have walked away or folded until times were better and people were in a position to start buying skis or skates or footballs again.

But not my father and uncle. They felt an obligation to the people who worked for them and to their families. Amazingly, not one of their employees was let go from work during the Depression. It wasn't until I was much older that I could appreciate the lengths to which my father and uncle went to insure that everyone at Newman-Stern stayed employed during that terrible time.

My mother's brand of caring – as you might expect from a "mom" – was somewhat more hands-on. To give you an example, each Christmas Eve while we were growing up, she would take Arthur and me to the family's store to gather up toys and equipment to take to our Hungarian relatives on the other side of town. That annual "Christmas expedition" became the heart of our holiday ritual.

So, can I say that my parents sat me down and showed me how to care, how to make charity a guiding principle in my life, how to be a philanthropist? Not really. But I did learn that caring only about oneself and one's immediate family is not enough when you are in a position to help others. And I learned it by example.

As an actor, I've often been asked to describe the process of creating a character. Acting is a question of absorbing other people's personalities and adding some of your own experience. If I had to describe philanthropy, I'd say the process is just the reverse. You start with your own experiences and from there you grow to embrace the needs of others.

In our office at Newman's Own, there's a brass plaque that reads "Assistant Life Guard on Duty." Like so much in this enterprise, it was hung as a joke. But there's a lot of truth there about our company's mission.

Philanthropy is about safeguarding and honoring life. It's about getting beyond ourselves and connecting with our "global family." Yet the simple, pure act of giving is so unusual today that people are baffled by it, and we wind up thinking it's more complicated than it really is.

Smart Generosity is a great little book. It brings our understanding of the act of philanthropy back to its simplest roots, and reinforces that very human impulse within each of us to take better care of each other.

More than that, Smart Generosity teaches us how to act on that giving impulse in a responsible and objective manner – with a view toward making a lasting difference.

A significant portion of Newman's Own charitable contributions have gone into setting up recreational camps for seriously ill children all around the world. If I ever had a doubt about whether this was an "investment" that made sense, that doubt is long gone. You create something where the children are to be the beneficiaries and find out that you get back a great deal more than you give.

No, I never planned to become a philanthropist. But it has been a tremendous ride – one that I'm proud to say my family has joined me on. I learned by the seat of my pants – and on the strength of a salad dressing that surprised itself into a corporate empire.

I wish Smart Generosity had been written years earlier – I could have used it. I'm delighted that it's here now and that I can share this book with friends, family, and colleagues who are searching for their own ways – more personal ways – to make this world a better place through wiser charitable giving.

* * * * *

Only days before the final manuscript for Smart Generosity was completed, Mr. Newman passed away. Although his accomplishments as an Academy Award-winning actor and successful racecar driver are the stuff of legend, it is his legacy as an innovative and unpretentious philanthropist that is his great contribution to humankind.

In 1982, he founded Newman's Own, a for-profit food products corporation that continues to donate fully 100% of its after-tax profits to charities around the globe. To date, the company's contributions total well over $250 million world-wide.

I am grateful and privileged to have received his permission to include the Foreword from Don't Just Give It Away in Smart Generosity. He will be deeply missed.

Smart Generosity

Preface

WHAT TOTAL AMOUNT WOULD YOU GUESS IS DONATED TO CHARITY in any given year?

**Over $300 billion is contributed to
nonprofit organizations annually
in the United States alone.**

**Individuals and families donate
more than $255 billion of that
in direct gifts or bequests.**

Do these staggering numbers surprise you? They should! Look around our communities, and across the nation as a whole – does it seem that $300 billion of "social progress" is achieved through the activities of the charitable sector each year? How much of that $255 billion (plus!) do you and your family contribute, and do you believe it is used as wisely as it could be?

* * * * *

Having worked and consulted within the charitable sector for nearly thirty years, I have witnessed the integrity and industry of the men and women of this sector who commit their lives – professionally or as volunteers – to make this world a better place for all of us.

Unfortunately, I could also tell you stories of waste and poor financial management that substantially eroded the value of our contributions – stories that never surface in the press or through the grapevine for fear that we will reconsider our charitable support.

In fact, I can guarantee that if you've ever made a charitable contribution, at least some small portion of that gift could probably have been used a little more effectively by the organization to which you gave it. Perhaps another charity would have accomplished a great deal more. And sadly, in some cases we might just as well have thrown our money away.

Like a leaking faucet that accumulates in wasted gallons, minor misuses of each of our charitable investments add up. In fact, they amount to huge amounts of donated money annually that could have – and should have – been applied to programs and services for the community...but weren't. And that's why we don't see $300 billion worth of progress from our contributions.

In the very best cases, that "leakage" of funds causes an organization to do just a little less than they otherwise could. In the worst cases, vital and urgent human needs of real-life men, women and children are going unmet – needs such as food, clothing, shelter, good health, education, and safety – because no one in the organization is truly "minding the store." Most cases fall somewhere in between.

How will this change? How can we as a community get our money's worth for our charitable contributions?

NONPROFITS MUST CHANGE

First, the nonprofit sector – collectively and as individual charitable corporations – must take their critical role in society far more seriously. This is particularly true for the volunteer leaders who are entrusted as board directors and trustees – the legal, financial, and moral guardians of our charitable sector.

And this is happening. The nonprofit community has looked itself in the mirror (and in The Wall Street Journal, and Forbes, and Fortune, and The Economist), and has re-doubled its efforts – particularly since the post-September 11th scandals – to become more accountable, more professional, and more effective.

The government is also doing its share in this effort. The Taxpayer Bill of Rights made it obligatory for the majority of charities to share their Form 990 financial information upon demand. Certain Sarbanes-Oxley measures now apply to nonprofits, and, with back-up from the IRS, government has forced boards and administrators to approach issues of compensation, self-dealing, and conflict of interest with greater deliberation.

Nonprofit leaders, too, are applying themselves to strengthening the sector through professional development. They are increasingly seeking technical assistance and education – training in nonprofit management, fund development, governance, strategic planning, program development and outcomes evaluation. In fact, academic degree and certification programs in fundraising and philanthropic administration are flourishing.

And finally – slowly but surely – board trustees are approaching their fiduciary responsibilities with ever greater seriousness.

WE AS DONORS MUST CHANGE

But the bottom line is still…the "bottom line." Whoever controls the bottom line has the greatest power – perhaps the greatest responsibility – when it comes to effecting constructive change.

And in the charitable sector, it is donors, givers, and philanthropists who ultimately control the bottom line. If you give to charity, you have the power to make the charitable sector more effective.

There is value in most every type and amount of charitable contribution. The more wisely the giving decision is made, the more valuable – and effective – is the gift.

To donate wisely – and therefore more effectively – we must take better control of our giving, and assess "charitable investment" opportunities as carefully as we would any other financial investment opportunity.

By working more closely with the nonprofit community, and making our giving choices more critically, we as individual donors and philanthropists can:

- Increase the economic impact of both our personal and combined charitable contributions,

- Improve the quality of life in our communities and around the world, and,

- Find a deeper personal satisfaction in charitable giving than we ever imagined.

This book will show you how.

PART ONE

GIVING, CHARITY AND PHILANTHROPY: THERE IS A DIFFERENCE

WHY A GUIDE TO "PHILANTHROPY"?

"Oh, Pookie, you're going to have such a hell of
a lot of fun with the foundation when I'm gone!"
— Vincent to Brooke Astor before his death

WHY A BOOK ON "PHILANTHROPY"?

"WHAT IS THE MOST SATISFYING GIVING EXPERIENCE YOU'VE EVER HAD?" Having asked this question hundreds of times over the last two decades, the varied responses still never fail to amaze and move me. Yet I am struck by how very, very rarely these highly personal stories involve conventional forms of giving to charitable organizations.

Ironically, many of the individuals least satisfied by their charitable giving are among the most prominent, visible, and generous financial contributors to nonprofits within their communities.

How is it that hundreds of billions of dollars are being channeled to charities world-wide each year by millions of donors, and yet so few donors feel a deep and abiding satisfaction from their financial contribution?

Put more simply, why does it seem like no one is having much fun in philanthropy anymore?

Yes, there are lots of galas, auctions, raffles, car washes, and cookie-thons. And a great deal of pleasure is had by all – in fact, it's such a good time, you'd hardly know it was "charitable" at all! Like "fat free" ice cream, we enjoy it despite the fact that it's supposed to be good for us.

A CHANGE IN MEANING

When society used to speak of "philanthropy," economic barons from another era – like Andrew Carnegie – would to come to mind. And we could point to a concrete impact they had on our world – forging a nationwide library system, for example.

Over time, however, there has been a subtle shift in our notion of a philanthropist. We still identify philanthropists as a class of "economic barons," but we find it a little harder to identify exactly what they have accomplished for society. And we have come to question their motives.

In fact, today's cynics would have us believe that a "philanthropist" is typically a stock-wealthy social icon, corporate statesmen, or technology entrepreneur who thinks he knows what's better for all of us.

Or put another way, a "philanthropist" is anyone with "a lot of money" who gives some of it away – and if they score a few PR points for themselves, all the better.

Depending, then, on how you define "a lot of money" and whether you give any of it away, you've probably already decided whether you are or could ever be a "philanthropist."

I've written this book to remind all of us that ANYONE can be a philanthropist, in the truest meaning of the word — and that being a philanthropist can and should be one of the most genuinely human and satisfying experiences or aspects of life. For – to paraphrase Millie Thornton, – philanthropy is a principle, not an amount.

How to begin? This book will show you HOW to become a philanthropist, from A to Z, regardless of your economic means.

WHAT THIS BOOK IS **NOT**

This book is NOT intended to convince anyone of the importance or value of giving. That is a decision that you have already arrived at alone, with your family, with your fellow board members, or with your legal and financial advisors.

This book is NOT about the various legal structures or vehicles through which philanthropic gifts can be made. It is not about the financial incentives of philanthropy for high net-worth individuals. It is not about building better community relations – even global community relations – through targeted corporate philanthropy.

This book is NOT designed to lead you to give more or less generously, or to more or fewer causes, or to any specific causes. Or to change your mind about the giving in which you are already engaged.

SO WHAT **IS** THIS BOOK ABOUT?

If you are going to give to charity, you should give with enthusiasm and derive a great deal of heart-felt satisfaction in the act, for through philanthropy, you do make the world a better place for all.

But when it comes to making your charitable investments, don't just GIVE it away!

This book is about approaching philanthropic giving as thoughtfully and insightfully – and personally – as you approach your financial investing.

This book is about a personal re-definition of philanthropy. And, it is about learning how to give with genuine enthusiasm – an enthusiasm rooted in the conviction that you can provoke positive, meaningful change in this world!

In essence, it is about making a fundamental change in the role you, your family, or your business play in your community and in the family of mankind.

BACK TO THE "REAL WORLD"

> *"Giving away money effectively is almost*
> *as hard as earning it in the first place."*
> — Bill Gates

If you're tempted to stop reading, let me reassure you – this is no "Zen and the Art of Giving." It is a practical, "how to" primer.

You've been careful in securing your future and that of your business – now what will you do with the rest of the money? This book will teach you how to make as careful an "investment" decision with your charitable giving as you did in your personal financial planning.

HOW DO I KNOW IF THIS BOOK IS FOR ME?

Whether you are newly committed to the idea of philanthropy, or looking for greater satisfaction from your charitable giving, or seeking assurance that your contributions are being used as effectively as possible, this book IS for you.

If you still have any doubts, review these stories of other folks who found the information in this book to be helpful and inspiring. Perhaps you'll meet someone whose story parallels your own:

1. **Your financial consultant or legal advisor has urged you to "get charitable" as a means of preserving your wealth, reducing your tax liability, or passing assets to your heirs intact.**

Bill and Marilyn,* a wonderful couple in their late 60's, was advised by their financial consultant that the establishment of a charitable remainder trust could solve their capital gains dilemma on a portfolio of highly appreciated stock. Moreover, the trust arrangement would accommodate the purchase of replacement life insurance that would guarantee their children's receipt of the equivalent full value of their parents' estate upon Bill and Marilyn's death.

The couple's estate planning attorney drew up the necessary documents, but when it came time for them to name a required beneficiary charity, they were lost. They had been so busy working and raising their family that they had never had the opportunity to get involved in charity, and now were being asked to donate the fruits of their life's work to one of hundreds of

* *Names have been changed to respect the privacy of the individuals involved.*

thousands of causes. Using the guidelines in this book, Bill and Marilyn were able to uncover a shared passion for a little-known cause. Childhood sweethearts, they decided to honor the town where they met and grew up by selecting a charity in that community. They followed the steps outlined in this book to assure themselves that their chosen charity had sound leadership and fiscal stability.

The unexpected satisfaction they experienced through this process inspired Bill and Marilyn to become involved with charitable work in their retirement community, something they never would have considered before.

2. **Your wise career choice and the wild success of your employer – or your own business - has placed you in a position of financial comfort you never imagined. In gratitude for your good fortune, you would like to "give back" to the community.**

Linda went to work for a "hot" computer software manufacturer right out of college. Although her salary would never make her "rich," she took advantage of the firm's generous employee stock option program. Eighteen years later, she was able to retire from the publicly-traded company. Having experienced the advantages of working in the technology industry, Linda decided that she wanted to apply some of her wealth to help at-risk kids access the opportunities in the high tech. field.

Where to start? Virtually every city and town in the country has a youth population in need. Should she apply her resources to groups working with children, teens, or young adults? Was it education, career information, or networking opportunities that would help fast-track Linda's successors into the field that had been so generous to her? By utilizing the tools and guides in this book, Linda was able to focus on those critical events in her own life that had opened the door for her to high-tech, and she was able to make clear decisions about how to use her charitable investment to help others step through that door, too.

3. **You have been involved in charitable giving for years, and are finding less and less satisfaction in sponsoring tables at the gala, holes at the golf tournament, or rooms in new buildings.**

Norm and his wife Marguerite live the comfortable country club life of many retired corporate executives. A generous pension, stock options, and very wise investing have given them the freedom to travel around the globe, and to entertain frequently at both their Midwest and Palm Springs homes. Norm's large network of top-level business colleagues, coupled with Marguerite's high social profile, place them at the top of every charity's A-list. About five years into retirement, Norm and Marguerite changed financial advisors. It was then that Norm and Marguerite realized, for the first time really, how much they had given over the years to charity, primarily through event sponsorships, silent and live auctions, charity sports tournaments, naming opportunities in new buildings, and countless ticket purchases to events they hadn't even attended. Norm, particularly, was astounded. He realized he never would have made business investment decisions the way he and Marguerite had been making their charitable investments. They decided as a couple that they had endured enough balls, auctions and tournaments to last a lifetime. It was time to invest their contributions in a more business-like manner. As charity was a new "business" to both Norm and Marguerite, they sought the professional counsel of their financial advisor and the guidance offered in this book to re-structure their charitable giving. Norm now understands that the profit and nonprofit worlds are not so far part: market assessment, strategic planning, committed and knowledgeable leadership, quality programs and service, relevant evaluation methodologies, and sound fiscal and investment policies are the hallmark of every successful nonprofit. Norm is enjoying applying an investment perspective in making the final family giving decisions while Marguerite has learned how better to listen to her heart in setting the family's charitable course.

4. **You receive many more requests for contributions than you could possibly respond to positively – you would like to say "no" without feeling guilty.**

Nancy's name recently appeared in a local publication as one of the top philanthropists in her community. She had more requests than she could respond to even before the article came out. Now she is flooded with calls and letters, and most of the requests are for truly worthy causes. Nancy woke up many nights overwhelmed with guilt about all the people she couldn't help, and wondering how she could say "no" without feeling so badly about it. She reviewed the principles outlined in this book.

Once she understood why and how an effective philanthropist MUST say "no," and how to make the wisest decision about how and when to say "yes," Nancy was able to become a more powerful force for positive change in her community – gaining admirers and emulators in the process.

5. **Your family or business has decided to consolidate its charitable giving through the establishment of a foundation.**

Ed had built a multi-national corporation through a brilliant strategy of acquisitions and mergers. Over the years, many organizations in the company's hometown had asked for contributions for a local cause. Early on, the requests had come to Ed's office directly, and he'd often write a check out of his own account. Soon, Ed became too busy to deal with non-business-related matters, and had his secretary pass requests for help to the human resources manager. As the company grew, human resources could no longer deal with charity pleas, and the responsibility was turned over to the new community relations department. Now, the requests no longer came from just the home office community. With each new merger or acquisition, charities from those communities joined the ranks of those applying for funding. With no cohesive policy on giving, there was no way to track whether the gifts served or supported the company's mission, or whether the funds even had any truly positive impact on the community.

In the interest of good corporate citizenship, Ed and his board of directors decided to consolidate the company's giving activities through the establishment of a corporate charitable foundation. Through the foundation, the firm is now making substantial grants that benefit the communities around the world where their employees and clients live and work. They have been able to link nonprofits from different communities to share innovative approaches, and through targeted funding have facilitated collaborations on a local level. Most importantly for Ed, the foundation serves as a focal point of unity, strength, and a common mission for the many diverse divisions and cultures represented in his multi-national operation. The principles and approaches outlined in this book shaped that corporate foundation.

6. **Your spouse or partner used to receive and handle all of the requests for contributions – it's now become your responsibility.**

Barbara and Barry ran a successful business operation that grew to a multi-entity corporation. Over the eighteen years of their marriage, they made many charitable contributions. Barry, as the more visible partner in the business, received most of the requests and made most of the giving decisions. An ugly divorce resulted in a split of the business. Barry bought out Barbara's share. Word spread that her settlement was large, and Barbara became a prime target for charities throughout the community. She was besieged by requests for money and time, requests she had never handled before. Her financial advisors offered little guidance in this area, often suggesting that Barbara merely follow the patterns of giving that Barry had established. Barbara needed to take some time to re-examine her personal priorities and get acquainted with the work and needs of the charities approaching her. Then she had to start making some tough financial decisions about which groups to support. The principles in this book guided her through this process.

7. **You sit on numerous charity boards and are asked to serve on many more than you can accommodate. You would like to insure that your investment of time, energy, expertise and money is directed where it can have the greatest impact.**

Monica's family name is well-known nationally both in the business and charity communities. Many nonprofits have asked Monica to serve on their boards, promising that little would be expected of her given her hectic schedule. These charities believed that just having Monica's name on the letterhead would bring credibility – and hopefully a contribution from her family's coffers – to the organization. Once Monica realized that spreading her name so thinly diluted its value to all of the charities, she decided to pare back and give her full attention – and generous financial support – to only two nonprofits per year. She asked each organization to prepare, in essence, a proposal for her support. Using the information and questions in this book, she made an objective selection of her first two beneficiaries, and has continued to play an important role in the accomplishments of those two groups ever since.

8. **You recognized yourself as "the millionaire next door" – and realized that charity that "starts at home and stays at home" may harm your children more than it helps.**

Jim and Florence married when he returned from WWII's Pacific theatre. Jim worked as a teacher and Florence as a secretary. They raised two sons and a daughter, all the while dutifully putting 15% of their earnings in savings. When Florence's parents died, they left their estate – including a home and some investments – to Jim and Flo. The couple decided that hard work, their focus on family, and shared goals and values were the greatest legacy they could pass to their children. They were concerned that passing the windfall to their offspring, now in their 30's, would deprive the young people of the opportunity to find their own paths and meet their own challenges, as Jim and Florence had.

They made arrangements for the eventual financial comfort of their children, and then decided to invest in charities that would benefit their grandchildren. Not knowing where to start, they took the steps outlined in this book to guide them.

9. **Your recent lottery win, inheritance, or appearance in a major publication has brought a flood of requests for charitable contributions and you do not know how to respond or react.**

Sharon's fast-growing homemade food company was featured on the business page of the city newspaper. Overnight, community groups from throughout that region of the state began writing and calling to request sponsorship funds and program grants – from food banks to Girl Scout troops. She knew that some of these organizations could help bring her company even more recognition – and sales – but wasn't sure how to guarantee that her company got the mileage she wanted from these charitable contributions. The tips in this book helped her understand what to look – and ask – for.

10. **You have no heirs, and would like to use your fortune to leave a meaningful legacy.**

Ruth had never married and had no children. As an only child with virtually no extended family, she realized that with her passing, the family name would vanish. She decided to leave her estate to a charity that would agree to name a room or building wing in her family's honor. Where to start? In the port city that welcomed her immigrant parents, her current home town, the city where she attended college? How did one go about finding a building looking for a name? How could she be sure the name would continue to be used? The step-by-step question-and-answer format of this book led Ruth to her answer.

BEFORE YOU BEGIN. . .

This book provides a comprehensive guide to defining your personal, family or corporate philanthropic focus. It also outlines a step-by-step process for identifying and assessing charitable organizations and programs that meet the philanthropic guidelines that you develop.

The manner in which you choose to structure, convey, or time a charitable gift is not a subject for this book. That is a matter best discussed and determined with your professional financial and legal advisors.

I invite you to look at philanthropy in a whole new light . . .

୨୦

CHAPTER 1

୨୦

GIVING AND GETTING

"Giving should be entered into in just the

same careful way as investing...

Giving is investing."

—John D. Rockefeller

I NVESTING IN CHARITY IS NO DIFFERENT THAN INVESTING IN THE MARKET. It is a proactive process of defining your investment goals and identifying opportunities that will lead to those goals.

Yet a substantial amount of "charitable giving" today is approached as casually as the purchase of a lottery ticket. The brief satisfaction of the contribution outweighs whether or not any specific or measurable "investment" goal was achieved.

A lottery ticket may cost only $1.00. But many philanthropic donations being made today range from less than $100 to well over $1 million – with shockingly little attention being paid to real outcomes.

Each year, in the U.S. alone, nearly one million charities solicit and secure over $300 billion in contributions from individuals and corporations. Do the donors get their money's worth? To put it more personally, have you gotten your money's worth? And, how would you know whether you did?

What did you expect to result from your gift? What did you expect as an outcome? Much of that will depend on what motivated you to give in the first place.

WHO GIVES AND WHY?

Charitable donors can generally be separated into four major categories: the "social" donor, the "quid pro quo" giver, the "conscience" contributor, and the true philanthropist.

THE "SOCIAL" DONOR

The social donor – also known among fund-raisers as the "vanity" giver – places a high value on the personal visibility and social prestige his or her contribution will bring. Such donors also place great importance on interacting with other high-profile community leaders and public figures. The fact that their funds may influence a constructive change in the community is secondary in the donor's evaluation of the investment.

In one example of a "social" gift, an East Coast newcomer to a high-net-worth retirement community on the West Coast contacted our firm for information on the major charities in this southern California desert resort. When asked about his charitable interests, the gentleman replied he had none. He just wanted to get acquainted with the town's wealthy movers and shakers as quickly as possible and knew the charity route was the fastest way to accomplish that end.

Charitable gifts from this category of donor are primarily mid-sized to very large – depending on who else is at the table. "I'll see you – and raise you" is not an uncommon attitude. The expected return on investment is prominent recognition and the opportunity to socialize on a regular basis with contributors of a similar social or economic class. Rarely does the donor require the nonprofit to "document" the institution's use of the "investment," or to report on the organization's performance as impacted by the contribution.

In another example, a major real estate developer was having difficulty in getting what he felt was a "fair hearing" on his controversial new project. He investigated the city councilpersons' charitable involvements, and discovered that a majority of them happened to belong to a cultural institution's auxiliary group. He immediately "bought" a high-level membership in the support club. A key benefit of membership was frequent social gatherings and "preview" cocktail parties at which this small group of supporters could mingle and chat. It was the perfect opportunity for the developer to meet his adversaries informally and off-the-record to talk up the benefits of his project - while serving the charitable interests of the community at the same time. The developer, by the way, never cared what the organization did with his money. He felt he got what he paid for: access to individuals who would have a major influence on the success or failure of his business dealings.

THE "QUID PRO QUO" GIVER

The second category of donor is the "quid pro quo" giver. These contributors generally donate to organizations in which a close friend or colleague is involved. The nature of the subject nonprofit is almost irrelevant. The contribution is based on a respect for or trust in the person making the request.

A few years back, I was sharing a working lunch with the capital campaign chair of a children's organization. We were dining at his private country club when an older gentleman approached our table and gave my companion a hearty greeting. When asked what the campaign chair was up to these days, he replied, "Oh, we're trying to build a new museum." As the gentleman continued to his own table, he remarked over his shoulder, "Put me down for fifty." In twenty years of experience, that was the fastest $50,000 commitment I'd ever witnessed. And it was made solely on the basis of the trust and respect felt for the capital campaign chairman.

In another type of quid pro quo gift situation, there is often the unspoken understanding that the donor may request a contribution for his or her own favorite charity in the future.

At more than one donor prospect rating meeting I've heard charity volunteers say, "I gave $10,000 to his pet charity, he owes me. I know I can get at least ten back out of him." In many circles, charitable contributions have become a social currency, a "debt marker" of sorts. And in these situations, as with vanity giving, return on investment is rarely measured in terms of organizational outcomes.

THE "SOCIAL CONSCIENCE" SUPPORTER

The third category of donor is the "social conscience" supporter. These are persons who give to one or more organizations because they truly or deeply believe in the importance or urgency of the nonprofit's mission. The donor may or may not have a personal connection with the agency, but will respond to a reasoned and impassioned request that touches his or her own concerns.

The most common form of conscience giving is via response to a direct mail request. Most often, the request will come from a well-established or highly credible charity, either national or very local in scope. It may be from the Sierra Club, the American Cancer Society, Amnesty International, or the local Cub Scout pack. The donor responds because of a general conviction that the work of the organization is vital, and that the leadership of the charity will use the contribution wisely – and there is a track record to support these assumptions.

A conscience contributor is not unlike the small-time investor who buys blue chip stock because they trust – without knowing a lot of details – that it will perform well.

Despite general familiarity with the mission, the conscience contributor can seldom list for you the specific initiatives or programs which are sponsored by the charity. And they rarely know – or particularly care – about exactly how their contribution was used or what measurable impact it had. This is true, in large part, because such a donation is usually relatively modest in size.

THE PHILANTHROPIST

The final category of charitable contributor is the focus for this book – that is, the "philanthropist." In contemporary parlance, "philanthropist" has come to describe anyone of wealth who gives any of it to charity. What an injustice to the true philanthropist!

In short, philanthropists are those contributors who carefully invest their wealth in the nonprofit sector specifically in order to benefit the general good of mankind, and to effect substantive positive change in the world.

Unlike givers in the preceding three categories, the philanthropist – whose contribution may range from mid-size to mega-gift – will be most interested in how and to what degree his or her contribution has had a profound, lasting, and measurable impact on some particular social challenge.

The best-publicized gifts of contemporary philanthropy have been those of enormous financial magnitude. A benchmark in philanthropy was set in 1995 when the late Walter Annenberg, former U.S. Ambassador to the Court of St. James, donated $500 million to public education in an effort to improve school systems nationwide. Specifically, his gift was intended to "challenge the nation to renew its faith in public education by redesigning and reforming its schools by the year 2000."

The Annenberg Challenge was followed by that of broadcast magnate Ted Turner, who pledged $1 billion over ten years to the United Nations in support of its worldwide relief and charitable activities. Turner's philanthropic commitment had a double objective. Immediately apparent was the desire to improve the living conditions of the underserved and at-risk – particularly children – across the globe.

Less obvious was his deliberate intent to provoke fellow billionaires, such as Bill Gates and Warren Buffett, to follow his philanthropic example – but almost a decade would pass before Gates and Buffett would make global headlines by combining their charitable assets.

In July 2006, Berkshire Hathaway mogul Warren Buffett made what was intended to be – literally – a world-changing commitment. He would begin transferring his vast personal fortune to five foundations. The lion's share, estimated at $31 billion, would pass to the Bill and Melinda Gates Foundation, more than doubling in size the world's wealthiest foundation.

Arguably the nation's savviest and most successful investor, Buffett absolutely expects a return for this charitable outlay. He shares the Gates' core belief that it is possible to improve health, reduce extreme poverty, and increase access to technology in developing countries in specific and measurable ways. It is this expectation – not the astonishing size of the gift – that defines his act as one of true philanthropy.

To more fully understand the notion of philanthropy – or philanthropic investment – one needs to appreciate the fundamental differences between giving, charity, and philanthropy.

GIVING, CHARITY, AND PHILANTHROPY

"Too many have dispensed with generosity
in order to practice charity."

-Albert Camus

Philanthropy is a state of mind – optimistic, determined, energized, and creative. Philanthropy is entrepreneurial. In fact, some of the world's most effective philanthropists were successful business entrepreneurs and visionaries. The same talents, insights and drive that fueled their business successes also made them great philanthropists.

Giving, charity, and philanthropy. These three words are often used interchangeably, yet even "charity" and "giving" have an unmistakable, albeit subtle, difference in meaning. And "philanthropy" is an act quite apart from either simple giving or charity, for philanthropy demands results.

GIVING

What does it mean when we "give" something? We give it "away." The act of giving suggests the one-way transfer of a tangible or intangible asset that holds a perceived value for the recipient. There is no expectation that the "giver" will receive anything in return.

For example, "I gave at the office" has become a dismissive phrase meaning "I already threw money (away) at that cause or issue." In the retail business, we often refer to "giveaways," incidentals.

With giving, the specific donation is often forgotten soon after – by both parties, the giver and the recipient.

Examples of "giving" include the change tossed in the donation can at the grocery store check-out, the check sent in response to a direct mail request by a local organization, or the weekly contribution dropped in the basket passed at church. In each case, there is an implied agreement that the money will be applied in a way most useful or beneficial to the recipient – specific usage is not keenly important.

CHARITY

"Charity," as its Greek and Latin roots suggest, is a gift given out of love. In "charity," there is an implied empathetic or emotional relationship, however brief, between the donor and the beneficiary. Most often, an act of charity is an acknowledgment of need or pain on the recipient's part.

As with "giving," there is no expectation of an exchange, or a return of some tangible sort, to the benefactor initiating an act of charity. The "good feeling," and faith that the pain or need will be diminished to some degree, is considered reward enough.

An act of charity, however, implies an inequality. There is an underlying understanding that the benefactor is the "have" and the beneficiary is the "have not." The relative social (and moral?) inequality of the two parties is unmistakably implied. That is why the notion of "charity" is almost considered a bit too "Dickensian," a touch politically incorrect, by today's standards.

PHILANTHROPY

"Philanthropy" is a notion and act quite apart from "giving" or "charity." The word's Greek and Latin roots (from *philanthropos*) attest to the notion that philanthropy is motivated by a deep and abiding love of mankind. In its truest meaning, *philanthropos,* or "philanthropy," implies a deeply-felt conviction for the worth of all mankind.

The most effective acts of philanthropy are rooted in the belief that all men and women are truly equals, therefore deserving of the basic essentials of human existence or experience.

Although each philanthropist may define those essentials differently – e.g. a clean environment, sufficient food, exposure to art, safe and adequate housing, a basic education, the freedoms of speech and religion, good health – there is among all philanthropists a unifying respect for the community of man.

And, unlike "giving" or "charity," philanthropy demands response.

PHILANTHROPY is a calculated investment made with the expectation that humankind – or some small part of it – will be profoundly, measurably, and permanently changed for the better as a direct result of the contribution.

Clearly then, "philanthropy" requires vision, a specific notion of the world, or some small subset of it, as a better place. The importance of vision in philanthropy cannot be overemphasized.

"Philanthropy" demands patience and the knowledge that great change rarely happens in a hurry.

And effective philanthropy can only become engaged in the context of a plan, a roadmap for achieving or arriving at the vision.

It is not the dollar amount of the "gift" – or even the ultimate result – that separates a donor from a true philanthropist. It is intent, expectation, and vision that separates the two…not unlike the distinction between someone who "dabbles" in the market and a serious investor.

PART TWO

Defining Your Philanthropic Goals

CHAPTER 2

DRAWING ON YOUR PERSONAL HISTORY

*"In the quiet hours when we are alone and there
is nobody to tell us what fine fellows we are, we come
sometimes upon a moment in which we wonder,
not how much money we are earning, nor how famous we have become,
but what good we are doing."*

— A.A. Milne

WHEN A GROUP OF PHILANTHROPISTS WAS RECENTLY ASKED TO SHARE their most satisfying giving experiences, virtually none of the answers made reference to a financial contribution to a charity.

One elegant and well-humored lady known for her many generous contributions to charity wistfully recalled a special experience from her early childhood. She remembered the special pleasure she felt whenever her mother would hand-make a dress for her. It so happened that her closest school chum was an orphan who lived under much less fortunate circumstances. The young girl asked her mother if she would make a special dress for her friend, offering to forego a new outfit for herself if her mom would agree. She has never forgotten the experience of sharing that surprise with her friend.

Sadly, it seems that many high net worth individuals and families find themselves feeling socially obliged to "share the wealth," but have lost – or perhaps never experienced – a deep satisfaction, enjoyment, delight or sense of accomplishment in the act of giving. *Noblesse oblige* has become, for many, a burden disguised as charity.

A number of myths have sprung up around the "joy" of giving:

- **Myth 1:** There is a correlation between the amount of money an individual contributes to charity and the degree of satisfaction experienced in the giving.

- **Myth 2:** The kind and quality of gift recognition influences the donor's satisfaction in making the donation.

- **Myth 3:** There is a greater pleasure in giving as one gets older, or as one becomes financially capable of making ever-larger gifts.

As much as they may deny it, nonprofit organizations solicit contributions based on the assumptions that these myths are true. Yet in surveying individuals and families involved in charitable giving, the truth lies far from the myth.

The story of the gentlewoman who recalled the joy of sharing a new dress with her friend is not atypical of the experiences many philanthropists point to as their most gratifying. Most often, their greatest satisfaction came from a small act of kindness that stemmed from the heart, and was received – with overwhelming gratitude and innocence – by an unsuspecting recipient.

Another source of immense pleasure for donors is the gift that repays a small act of kindness that was deeply cherished by the now-philanthropist.

For example, young John Brooks Fuqua had an imagination and curiosity that couldn't be satisfied on the farm where he grew up. He wrote numerous letters to every library in the region asking if he might be allowed to check out books by mail. Only one library reached out to fill the young boy's hunger to read. Many, many decades later, multimillionaire philanthropist Fuqua repaid that small kindness with gifts totaling $37 million to Duke University – for it was the school's librarian that had responded to the young boy's plea.

Those donors who experience the highest degree of profound or long-lasting satisfaction in giving share a common approach to philanthropy: they are pro-active in targeting beneficiaries rather than reactive.

Most have consciously or unconsciously reviewed their own life experiences to uncover those moments or incidents that most dramatically altered the very course of their life. The incident, act, or experience may have been a very positive one or perhaps a very painful one. But it is one moment that has never been forgotten.

The most satisfied philanthropists seek out individuals and organizations who are passionately and honestly working to bring the possibility of that experience – or the elimination of that experience – to others.

And if no one else is out there "doing it," the philanthropist will often create and fund his or her own initiative to enhance or protect the lives of others.

The philanthropist's experience of giving differs from that of the person who simply "donates." That difference is not unlike the difference in pleasure experienced by a craftsman who has hand-built his chair versus the shopper that picked one up at a department store.

WEALTH AND PHILANTHROPY

We spoke in the opening of this book about the myth that giving large sums of money makes one a philanthropist. Is there any correlation, then, between wealth and philanthropy? Indirectly, yes.

It is no accident that some of the most effective philanthropists are men and women who succeeded in business. The fruit of that success happens to be money.

The source, and engine, for that success, however, was vision. Very few individuals have become successful in a business, trade, or profession without a vision, a plan for achieving that vision, and the commitment to make that vision a reality. The status quo is never enough for these individuals.

Philanthropy, in its essence, requires vision – a vision of the world as a better place for the community of man.

Those who have the vision to succeed in business are also the ones that reap its rewards – wealth. When those same individuals turn their attention and their heart toward the vision of a better world, they have greater financial means than most to apply toward making that social vision a reality.

To put it more simply, the very attributes that made many philanthropists wealthy – vision and drive – are the same attributes that make these individuals "philanthropists" as opposed to just "donors."

These are, to a great degree, individuals who have never disconnected from their roots. They understand from experience that great things can be made to happen if you can, first, conceive of them, and second, focus your resources single-mindedly to making them happen.

This then is the link between wealth and philanthropy: vision.

WOMEN AND PHILANTHROPY

A great deal has been written recently about the differences in charitable giving patterns between men and women. A great deal has been speculated about why women seem to contribute less generously than men, why they take longer to make a giving decision, why they seem to spread their charitable contributions rather than concentrating them.

Where are the female Carnegies, Annenbergs, Gates, and Buffetts? Why are women more prone to buy the $10,000 gala tables while men endow the $1,000,000 chairs?

Socially, some reasons are quite obvious. First, women have, over the ages, had less independent capital to contribute. Secondly, until only the last generation or three, women have had limited control or input with respect to the family finances. And thirdly, as Gloria Steinem herself admitted, many women share the fear of becoming destitute or homeless –"bag ladies" – in their later years.

Quite simply, women have had neither the means nor motive to play a major role in philanthropy.

But there is another, less apparent but more compelling, reason why women do not wear the mantle of philanthropy comfortably.

Success in business requires vision. Entrepreneurship requires vision. "Practice makes perfect," the saying goes. Men – through business – have had the opportunity to assimilate – and exercise – the most essential attribute required by philanthropy: vision.

The business world is only now truly beginning to welcome women into the ranks of leadership and ownership. Until recently, women have simply not been in a position in society where "vision" was required, or even encouraged as an important attribute. "Vision" has been an under-developed talent for women of earlier generations.

Most women are only now, in the post-Eisenhower era, starting to look beyond home, the family, or a job promotion to "envision" a wealth of life, career and business possibilities.

With respect to business, more and more women are experimenting with and succeeding at entrepreneurship. They are gaining experience in conceiving, working toward, and achieving a long-term vision in the economic arena.

That experience – and the resultant financial wealth – is finally positioning women to play a far more significant role in the philanthropic community.

Again, wealth – a woman's independent wealth – and philanthropy are linked through vision.

FINDING A ROOT FOR YOUR PHILANTHROPY

"To give away money is an easy matter and in any man's power.
But to decide to whom to give it, and how large,
and when, and for what purpose and how,
is neither in every man's power nor an easy matter."
– Aristotle

So where do you begin your philanthropic journey? Begin with what you know – yourself. Take from the story you know best – the story of your life. In the moments of your life you will find that which has universal meaning: the experiences of love, pain, joy, discovery, loss, wonder, hardship, injustice, faith, triumph.

Recalling those moments isn't easy. Like watercolors, thirty, forty, seventy years start to "run" together, and those brilliant life-altering moments get lost in the great "wash" of time.

How do you re-discover them? Three simple methods are offered here to help you to uncover defining experiences of your life. Recalling those experiences can inspire and guide your philanthropy in directions you have never considered. Yet these may be the areas in which you will experience your greatest philanthropic satisfaction.

> *"It is by spending ONSELF*
> *that one becomes rich."*
> — Sarah Bernhardt

METHOD 1:
SIMPLY ANSWER THE QUESTIONS – SIMPLY

The answers to these questions are not of themselves intended to lead you directly to a personal philanthropic focus. Rather, they are designed to take you down some of the main roads of your personal history. Roads where you might just stumble upon a long-unexplored moment that altered – or could have altered – your life. Linger a moment and you just might discover that which inspires you to change the world. That is where to plant the root of your philanthropy.

By the way, don't waste this wonderful opportunity to share your story with someone older or younger who is special to you. Fix a cup of tea or coffee (or gin), turn down the phone, and share those key memories with someone who matters. They'll love really "seeing" you, and in opening your story up to others, you will be amazed at how many long-forgotten details re-emerge.

You also might consider digitally recording your reminiscences – your oral history can prove a rich resource later as you broaden your philanthropic horizons (and your family will treasure having this valuable keepsake).

CHILDHOOD EXPERIENCES

1. What are the four most specific moments you remember?
2. What were your three most positive experiences?
3. Which were the three most painful?
4. Where was your favorite place to go alone?

ADOLESCENCE

1. What were the biggest challenges and rewards of your adolescence:
   - At home?
   - At school,
   - With friends?
   - With the opposite sex?

5. Where was your favorite place to go alone as an adolescent?
6. Where was your favorite place to go with others?
7. With what adult outside your family did you spend the most amount of time?
8. Who was your favorite relative?
9. Who was your least favorite relative?

YOUNG ADULTHOOD

1. When was the exact moment that you first felt yourself an adult?
2. What were the circumstances of that flash of self-awareness?
3. What were your goals and dreams at 21?
4. What boosted you to reach those goals?
5. What blocked you from trying to achieve your dreams?

ADULTHOOD

1. At 35, what was your favorite place to go to alone?

2. What was your favorite place to go to with the important people in your life?

3. What periods of your life brought you the greatest stress or anger?

4. What experiences inspired your greatest joy or insight?

5. What significant crises or losses have you faced?

6. What was the single greatest surprise of your life?

50, 70 AND OLDER

1. At each of those benchmark ages, what was your greatest desire?

2. What was your greatest regret?

3. What was your greatest need?

4. What is the most important life lesson you wish you could share?

5. For what, specifically, would you like to be remembered?

EXPLORING THE WORLD

1. What three life experiences most altered your world view?

2. Describe your first experience in a foreign country or city.

3. What amazed you?

4. What saddened you?

5. What would draw you back there?

6. What would keep you from returning?

KEY PEOPLE IN YOUR LIFE

1. Who were the individuals in life who stopped to really get to know you?

2. Who passed you by when you needed them most?

3. Who was the first person of another race that you met?

4. Who was the first person from another country that you met?

5. Who was the first person of another faith that you met?

6. What were they like?

METHOD 2:
THEY COULD WRITE A BOOK ABOUT MY LIFE

You have been approached by an author who would like to write the story of your life, the definitive biography.

You agree – on one condition. You will provide the title for each chapter, and you will write the opening and closing paragraphs for each one as well.

The author enthusiastically accepts your condition, and tells you that each chapter will cover ten years of your life, starting with your birth. You have one week to bring him the chapter titles, and the first and last paragraphs for each ten-year section.

Begin to write.

METHOD 3: DO AS I DO... OR, FIND A PHILANTHROPIC ROLE MODEL

Many years ago, a wise man was teaching his daughter to swim. Stroke, kick, breathe, stroke, kick, breathe. She couldn't get the knack of it despite her father's coaching. It was too much to concentrate on at one time. Her legs and her arms seemed to want fight each other, and sputtering the horrible chlorinated water was the closest she could come to breathing rhythmically.

The father, realizing that the child would never learn to enjoy swimming this way, called her out of the water.

Pointing to a young woman gracefully stroking laps in the pool, he urged his daughter to just jump in the pool and "pretend you're her." She did just that, and ever since, she, too, has been a graceful and confident swimmer.

May these stories of philanthropists both anonymous and renowned inspire you to just jump in...

- Few know the story of Andrew Carnegie's passion for building libraries. As a boy in Pittsburgh, he and his brother spent hours with other working kids enjoying the 400-volume private library of a Colonel Anderson. When Carnegie grew wealthy, he never forgot what he termed the Colonel's "precious generosity" and committed his resources to establishing a network of free libraries across the nation that continue to stand today as one of the single greatest philanthropic undertakings of all time.

- Zachary Fisher, 86, was awarded the Medal of Freedom, the country's highest civilian honor. As a young construction worker in the late 1930's, he suffered a knee injury which disqualified him from service during World War II. He was devastated when he was refused induction in 1942 and never forgot the price that others paid to defend his freedom and that of the nation. He went on to become a successful developer. He has used his wealth to support the families of soldiers killed in the service of the country. In 1983, he sent a check for $10,000 to the children of each of the 241 Marines and service personnel killed in the bombing of a Beirut barracks to help pay for their college education. In 1989, Fisher sent $25,000 to the family of each man lost in the turret explosion aboard the battleship Iowa. He has sent another 600 checks of at least $10,000 to the families of other military personnel killed while serving. "I always felt that I owed something to the men and women who defended my freedom and allowed me to become so successful in such a great country."

- The late Joan Kroc, widow of McDonald's magnate Ray Kroc, was legendary for her generosity to charities and victims of disaster across the U.S. Her $80 million gift to the Salvation Army, however, was inspired by one of her fondest memories of her late husband - he would dress as Santa, ringing a bell for Salvation Army donations.

- Osceola McCarty, an 88-year-old laundress, gave her life savings of $150,000 to finance scholarships at a local Mississippi college. She had never enjoyed the luxury of an education.

- Famous talent agent Michael Ovitz repaid UCLA Medical Center for providing medicine for his child in the middle of the night with a gift of $25 million in Disney stock.

- Robert E. McDonough, founder of RemedyTemp, Inc., honored Georgetown University, his alma mater, with a $30 million multi-year contribution. McDonough believes the night-school education he got at

Georgetown while working Capitol Hill as a policeman in the 1940's laid the foundation for his later success in business.

- Far less dramatic experiences can also inspire philanthropic gifts. The memory of Maddie, his late schnauzer, was the inspiration for David Dufflefield, the Founder, President and C.E.O. of PeopleSoft Inc., to establish a $200 million fund for animal welfare organizations. The basis for his philanthropic passion: honoring Maddie, who was always there for him with "unconditional love" during the periods of greatest personal and professional stress.

SUMMARY

It is not impossible to regain the pleasure of giving. All it requires is searching one's own life experiences to find those that touched your soul. Then seek out individuals and groups who are passionately and honestly working to bring the possibility of that experience to others. Your hands, your heart, your laughter or tears engaged in that endeavor will bring you the joy of giving. Do what you love, then let the money follow.

CHAPTER 3

SELECTING A "SPHERE OF INFLUENCE" FOR YOUR PHILANTHROPY

"Apart from the ballot box, philanthropy
presents the one opportunity the individual
has to express his meaningful choice over the
direction in which our society will progress."
— George Kirstein

NOW THAT YOU HAVE IDENTIFIED OR NARROWED THE FIELD OF NEED or service in which you would like to provide support, your next mission will be to identify the "sphere of influence" within which you wish your philanthropy to have an impact.

Think of the "sphere of influence" as the circle or segment of society within which you can make a difference through your philanthropy. A good analogy for illustrating the concept of sphere of influence is our governmental structure.

A mayor's sphere of influence is his city, a governor's is her state. The President's circle of responsibility is the nation. The Secretary-General of the United Nations has within his or her sphere of influence much of the globe.

Within government, the larger your sphere of influence, to some degree, the more dilute is your power to have a profound impact within that circle. Unless, of course, you have a strong base of support and enormous resources.

The same is true in philanthropy. To make change – even constructive change – in society, the greater your resources and number of like-minded supporters, the more likely you will be to succeed.

The philanthropist's decision with respect to his or her chosen sphere of influence is a critical one. It is a decision that will be predicated in part upon:

- The choice of field(s) drawing the donor's passionate interest
- The size of investment the donor wishes to make
- How quickly the donor wishes to see a return on his or her investment

There are essentially four spheres of influence to choose from as a charitable donor. Within each, there may be sub-categories, and there is a great deal of overlap between these spheres, but the general circles of influence can be distinguished as follows:

- Personal or individual
- Community
- Institutional or infrastructural
- Policy

How does selection of a sphere of influence guide your charitable giving activities? Let's look at an example:

CASE:
MAKING CHANGE IN THE WORLD THROUGH EDUCATION

One small family foundation in a desert community of Southern California determined that academic opportunity had provided the key to success that led their family to prosperity. They decided to share their good fortune by making scholarships available to promising, low-income students in the family's hometown. Each year, they pay between partial and full tuition for a group of students who otherwise would not have the resources necessary to attend college, graduate school, a professional school or vocational institute. This family elected to engage their philanthropy at a very personal level, impacting individual lives as their method for changing the world.

Similarly, in 1997, philanthropists John Walton and Ted Forstmann donated $6 million to fund one thousand scholarships for low-income Washington, D.C., children to attend the private schools of their choice.

A donor in yet another part of the country elected to make his impact on a community-wide level. This individual chose to contribute $10,000 to an educational foundation benefiting all of the schools in a particular community. Although he could not trace the impact of his gift to a specific child – or even a specific school – he believed that the application of his resources would create an improved school environment for all students in that community.

But perhaps the most famous contemporary gift dedicated to impacting infrastructure through education has taken root in the Midwest. A small group of anonymous donors in Michigan have come together to establish an unprecedented initiative known as "The Kalamazoo Promise." The program, launched in 2005, guarantees full college scholarships to potentially every graduate of the Kalamazoo Public School district.

Unlike most scholarship programs, where merit and need are emphasized, the qualifications for participation in the Kalamazoo Promise are simple: continuous residency and enrollment in the city's public school district followed by admission to a State of Michigan public college or university, where a 2.0 grade point average must be maintained.

The educational objectives of the initiative are obvious: to lower the cost of post-secondary education, thereby increasing incentives for high school graduation, college attendance, and college completion.

The economic development benefits may be less apparent, but are even more profound in terms of the city's infrastructure. The scholarship program has already affected Kalamazoo's housing market and property values.

The Promise is aiding the city in attracting businesses seeking to invest, expand, or relocate. The "sales pitch" is simple – not only will employee families have access to free college tuition, but the businesses themselves will be able to tap an increasingly well-trained workforce.

Lastly, the arrival of middle-class professionals drawn by the initiative is revitalizing the city's downtown area. Retail and service merchants as well as cultural institutions can draw from a larger population capable of supporting a vibrant urban center.

Certainly, city of Kalamazoo is benefiting. More importantly, by applying resources to re-designing the school system in one city, a new model for public school reform and urban economic development has been created. The model of The Kalamazoo Promise is already being replicated in more than a dozen U.S. cities and could eventually be applied to public school districts throughout the country.

And, illustrating the fourth option for a sphere of influence, numerous private foundations engage in support of policy research institutes and "think tanks," such as the Educational Policy Institute or Education Sector, seeking methods by which our educational system can be improved through altering or amending legislation or public policy.

How do you determine which "sphere of influence" is right for your philanthropic giving? To a great degree, that will be determined by how important it is for you to "see" the impact of your giving. Do you expect to see a measurable change in a life or improvement in society within your lifetime?

IMPACTING INDIVIDUAL LIVES

By selecting to assist individuals as your sphere of influence, you would be choosing to use your charitable giving to immediately impact one or more person's lives. The impact on their quality of life may be permanent, temporary, or even momentary. Some examples:

- Scholarship aid
- Contributions of money or goods to food banks or homeless shelters
- Grants to individual visual or performing artists to encourage their work
- Donations to agencies offering support to elderly or sick individuals
- Underwriting delivery of pharmaceutical drugs or medical supplies to disaster-stricken or impoverished areas
- Funding the purchase of teddy bears for toddlers involved in domestic violence or abuse
- Making someone's "dying wish" come true
- Underwriting the telephone costs for a rape crisis or suicide hotline
- Purchasing bicycles for individuals in rural communities
- Donating books and supplies to a local adult literacy or vocational training program
- Subsidizing veterinary service costs for low-income families or older adults
- Sponsoring a mentoring program
- Gifting to hands-on human service agencies such as the Red Cross or the Salvation Army

The list of possible ways in which your philanthropy could directly – and measurably – touch and change individual lives is virtually endless. And such acts of generosity do not have to be restricted to your home community or even to the continent on which you reside.

IMPACTING A COMMUNITY

In a "community-focused" approach to philanthropy, the donor desires to use his or her charitable giving in order to improve the overall quality of life among a defined group of people. The community may be defined by geographic area, ethnic or racial heritage, age group, gender, or some other common attribute. Support is generally provided to an organization or agency already organized to serve the needs of that community. For instance:

- Supporting a locally-based cultural or natural history center
- Giving to a synagogue, church, mosque, meeting hall or faith-affiliated school
- Contributing to a senior citizens service agency
- Donating for a community park, playground, or youth activity center
- Subsidizing an ethnic dance or music group
- Underwriting construction of a cancer, AIDS, or emergency illness clinic
- Endowing a library foundation

In community-focused giving, it is often possible to trace the benefit or impact of the gift on individual lives, even though there is a strongly social aspect to the impetus for the gift.

IMPACTING AN INSTITUTION OR INFRASTRUCTURE

Focusing one's giving on an institution provides the philanthropist with the opportunity to have a profound impact on the life of a particular or unique institution, such as a:

- School
- Hospital
- Museum
- Zoo
- Nature conservancy

The underlying philosophy in selecting this sphere of influence is that by improving or strengthening a key or core institution, a number of lives will be improved or enhanced, although perhaps no one specific life will be improved in some measurable fashion.

We see this on a larger scale where philanthropists have supported nonprofit or non-governmental agencies, efforts, and social movements that have sought to reform or re-form "institutions" or infrastructure which they believe to be fundamentally flawed, immoral or inhumane, for example:

- UNICEF

- CIVICUS
- Amnesty International
- Greenpeace
- International Campaign to Ban Landmines
- Physicians for Human Rights
- CARE International

IMPACTING POLICY

Philanthropists involved in this sphere of influence support efforts that examine and encourage alternative approaches to complex social issues, particularly those that have their roots in the law, regulation, politics, or "codified" social custom. Donors seek to encourage social, legal or economic reform through research and lawful systems change. Common targets:

- Discrimination on the basis of race, sex, creed, color, or sexual orientation as it applies to housing, employment, or education
- Abrogation of basic human rights such freedom of speech or religion, or the freedom to congregate
- Denial of legal rights guaranteed under the Constitution
- Medical care reform

WEIGHING THE BENEFITS OF EACH "SPHERE OF INFLUENCE"

For those philanthropists wishing to see the fastest and perhaps most dramatic results from their giving, the individual sphere of influence is the most likely to provide the greatest level of satisfaction.

BENEFITING AN INDIVIDUAL

For example, providing tuition for a student who otherwise might not be in school allows you as the donor to know exactly how and for whom your money will be used. If you have done your "due diligence" before making the gift, you can be fairly certain that your contribution will have a profound, serious, and lasting impact on the life of that individual. You will also be able to track whether that investment provided a worthwhile, measurable philanthropic return: Did the child stay in school? How was their academic performance? Did they become someone who could contribute to the world in a way they otherwise might not have? Did they move into employment or a profession that would not have been an option without education? Did they go on to inspire, assist or nurture the educational aspirations of others?

Philanthropy, the "love for all mankind," is rooted in a vision for the world, a long-term vision. Philanthropy, therefore, invests for the long-term. By engaging as a donor within an individual-centered sphere of influence, you are sowing "seeds" for tomorrow.

In other words, the student given an otherwise unattainable educational opportunity today – in a classroom, or at home, or in the community – will enjoy the benefits of that opportunity not just today, but at that point in the future when today's opportunities will be seen as having been the building blocks for the future they have attained.

Even more simply, by positively impacting a child today, you create the possibility of a better world for all of us tomorrow.

STRENGTHENING A COMMUNITY

Focusing your philanthropy on a community-centered sphere of influence has some of the benefits of directly affecting individuals, while also providing for slow, measured, recognizable improvement in the overall quality of life of a community.

Leo Adler, a multi-millionaire magazine distributor, got his start selling papers on the streets of Baker City, Oregon, at the age of 9. He never moved away from the home where he was raised by his immigrant parents. When he passed away at age 98, he left an unexpected $20 million to Baker City and its 10,000 residents. From the Little League, to the library, to the local fire department, there does not seem to be an area of community life that Adler's largesse has not touched. In addition, the foundation he left behind made scholarships available to every graduate of the town's two high schools, as well as to residents seeking higher degrees or professional training. His philanthropy will have a profound effect on the entire community of Baker for generations to come.

Some philanthropists choose to benefit an entire community for somewhat "selfish" reasons (although, as we've pointed out, "philanthropy" by definition is an unselfish endeavor). They select the community where family, loved ones, or others of great personal significance or importance to them have established their home. By improving the life of the community as a whole, these philanthropists know that their family members will enjoy the benefits as well.

This holds true for a corporate "family" as well. PepsiCo's former chief executive officer, Roger Enrico added his 1998 salary (save $1) to the company's $1 million scholarship fund for the children of company employees earning less than $60,000 per year. Enrico regularly referred to these loyal employees as the company's "front line" and felt he and PepsiCo should invest their philanthropic funds where their company's "community" could benefit.

There is one additional benefit to engaging in community-focused philanthropy – whatever the make-up or definition of your selected "community." The more people individually touched by your philanthropy, the greater the legacy you leave. Just ask the people of Baker City, Oregon, or the children of PepsiCo's employees.

TARGETING AN INSTITUTION

Institutionally-focused philanthropy is, frankly, very closely related to community-oriented philanthropy: the institution and its beneficiaries are, in a sense, the target community. Depending on the fashion in which the donor chooses to support the institution, the impact can be immediate and visible, or it can be somewhat more subtle and less apparent to the public eye.

For example, the philanthropist choosing an institutional sphere of influence might elect to provide the capital funding for a new wing, or to establish an endowment to ensure the long-term viability of an important new program or service. The results of such a gift could be visible very quickly.

On the other hand, the philanthropist might choose to provide funding for critical operating expenses needed by a battered women's shelter. The benefits of such gifts are rarely visible to the general public, or even to the donors themselves. Yet without general operating and overhead funds (which will be discussed in detail in Chapter 6), most institutions – in fact, most charitable organizations – could not exist to do their work.

TACKLING INFRASTRUCTURE

The effort to affect a change in infrastructure is among the most daunting challenges that a philanthropist will ever face. Ambassador Annenberg's unprecedented gift of $500 million to improve the public education system in our nation within seven years was one of the most visible undertakings of philanthropy in the area of systems change that this country has seen. In examining whether this sizable investment had an effect on public education in general, one would not be able to look to an individual school, or even a school district or system, to determine the gift's impact. And the final assessment of the national effects of that investment would take nearly fifteen years, some time after the donation was made.

The stated objective of the Annenberg Challenge was "to reinvigorate a national educational reform movement" in the United States, and "provoke and support on a national scale a systemic and organized effort to reform the nation's schools."

Looking at our public schools, there is little evidence that the Challenge achieved its initial lofty objectives. Does that make the Annenberg gift a failed investment? You decide...the programs launched through his gift touched the lives of 1.5 million students and 80,000 teachers located across 35 states.

More importantly, the results of the Annenberg Challenge identified a more effective approach to changing the educational infrastructure of this country. It shifted attention to the district as the main unit of reform, raising the issue of what school districts must do to improve schools.

The Kalamazoo Promise, because its focus is on impacting the infrastructure of a very focused geographic location, has evidenced concrete results much quicker than the Annenberg gift. The scholarship program is proving to be a successful investment relative to its short-term educational objectives. It will take the efforts of many other philanthropists and activists – and some years – to monitor, evaluate and promote the long-term impact of the project with respect to economic development and urban re-vitalization. And even more time will pass before these gains can be promulgated and replicated in communities throughout the country.

The philanthropist embarking on a journey to transform infrastructure must have patience and be willing to accept that the impact of his or her contribution may not be apparent until long after the gift is made. This can be very frustrating for many newer philanthropists, just as it is for newcomers to the stock market. Frankly, most of us would like immediate proof that our investment is working.

IMPACTING POLICY

Devoting charitable funds to a policy-centered sphere of influence is among the most important, expensive, and long-term investments that a philanthropist may choose to make. In the policy arena, the philanthropist also has the least amount of control over the outcome of his or her investment. That is, constructive research may not, ultimately, result in a policy change.

THE SIZE OF YOUR STAKE

How much money you have to invest will also play a role in selecting your sphere of influence. Practically speaking, it is far less expensive to pay a child's tuition than it is to restructure the American educational system. It is cheaper to fund a volunteer-run literacy program than to build a library. It costs less to provide meals to the home-bound on holidays than to reform the agricultural economy of a third-world nation. It is more economical to pay for one man's lung surgery than to fund a cure for cancer.

ESTABLISHING A LEGACY

Lastly, you can use the "By whom do I want to be remembered?" test to help determine which sphere of influence will be most satisfying to you.

For example, would you like to be remembered and honored by an individual or individuals who for many years to come will gratefully acknowledge that they would not have had the opportunities they were given but for your generosity? If this is the legacy you wish to leave, than the individual sphere of influence would probably be most satisfying to you.

If it would mean more to you to have your name linked to a specific institution with which you had an important or significant relationship, or if you would like your legacy to be tied (inexorably!) with the future of that institution, than the institutional sphere of influence will be more attractive to you as a philanthropist.

Of course, you may wish later that your philanthropy had taken another form. Famed showman P.T. Barnum was a benefactor of Tufts University. When Jumbo, Barnum's famed circus elephant died, it was stuffed and enshrined at Tufts. The memorial "trophy" was destroyed in a fire, but was later re-created in bronze and ensconced in Barnum Hall. As might be expected, both Barnum and Jumbo have been the objects of much humor around that campus over the years. On second thought, that may be just the legacy the great entertainer intended to leave behind!

If you would like to be remembered by a town or community of people which holds a special place for you, then community-focused giving would be most suited to your style of philanthropy.

Lastly, except in rare instances will any one individual or foundation be remembered for or credited with spearheading a substantive social or policy change. The collaborative nature of such work, and the timeframe required for success in achieving social change does not lend itself to singular attribution. If name recognition is important to you, the policy sphere of influence may not feel very rewarding.

SUMMARY

It is now time to answer this important question: relative to your charitable financial resources, the form you wish your legacy to take, and the immediacy with which you wish to witness the results of your philanthropy, which sphere of influence is right for you?

Your careful consideration of this matter can help you achieve a greater personal satisfaction from your philanthropic investments.

᠊ᠬᠬᠬ᠊

CHAPTER 4

᠊ᠬᠬᠬ᠊

WHERE WILL YOU MAKE
YOUR MARK?

"The money was made in New York,
so I've given it back to New York."

- Brooke Astor

O NE OF THE MOST EXCITING CHOICES THAT A PHILANTHROPIST WILL make is the geographic region or area where he or she will make that philanthropic investment. And there are many reasons why one might chose a particular area over another.

The late television icon Johnny Carson, for example, donated $150,000 to the community center in Logan, Iowa, the town where his grandparents lived. As a child growing up in Nebraska, Carson would visit his grandfather, C.N. ("Kit") Carson, who was mayor of Logan from 1944 to 1948. In 2005, his estate donated $5 million to a hospital in Norfolk, Iowa, Carson's hometown from the age of eight until his graduation from high school.

The obvious choice would be to make one's charitable investment in an area or region close the donor's main residence. By investing close to home, the philanthropist may find it easier to monitor and assess the effectiveness of his or her charitable contribution.

However, there may be other factors that a prospective donor will want to consider before limiting themselves to "the neighborhood."

WHEN SIZE DOES MATTER

For example, a charitable investment in a small town is more likely to have a measurable impact than the same-sized contribution made in a large city.

Or, if one of your motivations as a philanthropist is public recognition, the level of your gift may have a far higher value in a smaller town or community than it would in a major metropolitan area.

There are other benefits, however, to making your philanthropic investment in a large city. For example, there seems to be a trend for urban challenges, problems, and opportunities to resonate out from the urban centers to suburban and outlying metropolitan areas, and ultimately to rural areas. That same pattern, to some degree, can be reflected in the effects of charitable giving. In other words, by successfully addressing a social issue or challenge in a metropolitan setting, the philanthropist may create a model or paradigm that will translate to outlying areas as well.

REGIONAL CONSIDERATIONS

Some philanthropists may elect to benefit a region rather than a specific city or town. For example, some may choose a remote, mountainous, or desert area for their philanthropic base, recognizing that organizations in isolated areas have a much harder time attracting philanthropic support than agencies based in metropolitan or major industrial areas.

The fact is, the economic realities of an area with no major corporate or industrial presence, and which is populated by families living at or below the poverty level, will have a very difficult time attracting major gifts or strong corporate support for its nonprofit community. Yet the social issues and challenges in an isolated region – issues of literacy, hunger, educational opportunity, health, nutrition, environmental hazards, to name a few – may be far more critical than those same or similar challenges in an urban setting.

Trying to benefit an entire state may be, understandably, difficult. Size and population are just two factors to consider. As you might imagine, it would be more reasonable (and less costly) to attempt to have an impact on the entire state of, say, Rhode Island, than to strive at effecting a comparable impact on the state of California.

Choosing a state focus for your philanthropy, however, is not without some strong merits. The fact is, there are some states that are more acutely suffering the key social and economic challenges plaguing our nation today than others, for example crime, poverty, unemployment, illiteracy, discrimination. In states that are making a concerted effort to address those challenges, the climate for a public/private philanthropic partnership might be especially conducive or welcoming to interested charitable donors. Another strategic approach to funding might be to weave a state-wide "safety net" linking agencies serving like client populations.

IT'S A SMALL, SMALL WORLD

With advances in telecommunications, travel, and technology, the world has become a smaller and smaller place...with the Internet, it has become a global village. Social and economic factors in one nation are no longer confined within its borders. Social change, social advances, and social challenges – not unlike political and economic influences – today spread quickly across the globe.

Just as a rapidly-expanding economy in China influences the market economies of the rest of the globe, just as political turmoil in the Middle East poses political challenges for nations around the world, philanthropic investments in one country or another can have a profound effect beyond the borders of that one nation.

Consequently many philanthropists are looking beyond ethnic allegiances and national borders to identify critical areas or regions in the world where their charitable investment can provoke constructive change not only in that community, but in other communities strategically linked to that base. For example, by providing philanthropic assistance to countries south of the United States borders, it might be possible to ease social and employment challenges within U.S. border communities where immigration has become a major social factor. For other examples of international giving, one need look no further than the geographic choices of George Soros and Bill Gates in order to see how philanthropy can incite a "domino effect."

BIG FISH, SMALL POND

In selecting a home base, a philanthropist should not ignore the desire to be recognized or acknowledged for his or her generosity. For that reason, should you choose to make your gifts in a small town or perhaps a rural area, one will probably establish a more visible legacy than will the philanthropist investing that same dollar amount of support in a major metropolitan area. Think about whether it would be more satisfying for you to be "a big fish in a small pond," or the opposite. Put another way, in all candor, how big of a "splash" would you like your gift to make?

For example, Charles and Peggy Pearce of Corsicana, Texas, donated their important collection of contemporary Western art to tiny Navarro College in Corsicana. Pearce, a Cornell University alumnus, decided not to contribute the artwork to his alma mater as he felt the collection would not be as important to the prestigious university as it would be to Navarro.

REAPING WHAT YOU SOW

Another consideration in establishing or selecting a home base for one's philanthropy is the whole question of whether you wish to "concentrate" your charitable investment in one area for the purpose of exacting the maximum effect for your money, or whether to " sprinkle " your giving in a variety of community settings and geographic areas in order to "seed" change across a broader base.

All of the above factors may and should have an influence on your decision when selecting a home base for your philanthropy.

To help you explore just some of your options, below is a list of the most frequently cited locations for one's philanthropic largesse:

- The town, city, state, region, or country where you were born
- The place where you spent your early child
- The location where you attended grammar school
- The community where your high school was located
- The college town of your youth
- The place where you spent family vacations
- The city or town that was your first "home away from home"
- The home of your grandparents, favorite aunt and uncle, or other important people in your life
- The place you fell in love
- The city or town where you were married
- The area most closely identified with your family tree
- The place where you made your fortune, or your philanthropy found its footing
- The neighborhood where your children were born
- The town or city where your grandchildren or great-grandchildren currently live
- The place where you have retired, are planning to retire, or consider your second home
- An area that delighted or moved you on a visit
- A place that you read about, or learned about on television, in a movie, or on the Internet
- A location that you have dreamed of visiting one day (here's your chance!)

OFF THE MAP

One adventurous philanthropic couple decided that it would be great fun to become anonymous angels for an unsuspecting community where they had no prior connection. They selected the beneficiary town by opening an atlas of the United States, and, with eyes closed, simply pointing. They then repeated the "search" process using the appropriate state map.

The couple took a short trip to the town to see it for themselves, then began contacting the local community foundation and other umbrella services agencies for more in-depth information on the town's needs. They quietly researched the charities in the area to determine which seemed to be operating most effectively. As they learned about specific programs or services that were having a positive impact on the overall life of the community, they channeled substantial contributions to them.

They kept their secret closely, never revealing their identity to the many charities they endowed. And they delighted in their "sleuthing" almost as much as they did in their philanthropy.

SUMMARY

Choosing a home base for your philanthropy can be great fun and a way to honor, remember, or re-pay a community or place for the role it plays or played in your life or in the life of someone important to you. Don't let geography or distance limit your options. Chapter 7 will show you how to find worthwhile charities in whatever part of the country or world you choose, without having to stray much further than your telephone, mailbox, or computer.

CHAPTER 5

RISK AND RETURN: DEFINING YOUR "COMFORT ZONE"

"The trouble is, if you don't risk anything,
you risk even more."

- Erica Jong

JUST AS WITH ANY OTHER FORM OF FINANCIAL INVESTMENT, SOUND philanthropic investment requires an assessment of one's comfort level with "risk."

Where is the "risk" in philanthropy? It lies in how effectively your contribution will be used by a given organization to accomplish the specific charitable objectives you have set. More specifically, "risk" is determined by how capable an organization is of using your donation to make the greatest possible impact on the area of service that is your focus.

Your charitable contribution to one nonprofit can have more or less risk associated with it based on several factors:

- The organization's stage of development
- The size of the charity
- The nonprofit's budget

Just as with traditional investing, making your contribution to a "venture" organization – one that is new, young, or initiating a dramatically innovative program – has more inherent risk than donating to a large, well-established, older nonprofit of the "blue chip" variety.

In return for assuming the risk, however, you may gain the ability to have a greater impact with a smaller overall contribution. For example, newer, "venture" nonprofits frequently have lower overhead and tend to expend a higher percentage of their funds on service. The downside is the uncertainty of whether the organization will survive, much less thrive, over the long term. Should it fail, your contribution will have suffered the risk of having had only a momentary effect.

For example, donating $5,000 to a new charity run by volunteers with an annual operating budget of $10,000 can have a substantial impact on the their ability to provide services – if those services are well-planned and well-executed. But if the organization goes out of business eighteen months later, will you feel that you made a poor investment?

On the other hand, the "safer" the investment – with an established organization with a track record of service – the more reason you have to believe that your contribution will be used effectively. Further, you can feel fairly secure that your investment will serve as a "building block" along the charity's already established foundation of success.

Although your investment risk is lower, the immediate impact of your donation may be diminished by the larger scale of operations. That is to say, your $5,000 will have less of an impact on an operation whose overall program and service budget is $5 million or $25 million than it will on a small "venture" charity.

Put another way, the "safer" the investment, the more certain one can be that there will be a positive and longer-term return on that investment. However, that return may be incrementally smaller. For example, an organization such as the Red Cross is well-established, and has a well-publicized, successful track record. A donation to the Red Cross may not have as profound an impact in the larger scheme of its overall activities, but you can feel secure (at lower risk) that your contribution will be soundly utilized.

THE "LIFECYCLES" OF A NONPROFIT
"In all things there is a law of cycles."
- Tacitus

Virtually every non-profit or charitable organization will move through three distinct phases over the course of its lifetime. At each stage of its development, the organization will have unique needs, unique challenges, and unique opportunities. Also at each stage, the nonprofit will pose unique challenges and offer a unique potential for return. By determining an organization's position in its cycle of development, the philanthropic investor can more accurately assess the potential risks and rewards of contributing to that charity. In this chapter, the "lifecycles" of a charitable organization will be examined.

THE "EMERGING" STAGE

The first stage of development is the "emerging" or grass roots stage. This is that critical one- to two-year phase immediately following the launch of a new charity. This phase is marked by several distinctive characteristics.

Generally, the newly-formed organization is headed by its founder, who is someone with a very strong vision, and the energy and will try to make that vision a reality.

The leadership of the organization at this stage generally comprises a relatively small group of like-minded people who subscribe to the founder's mission and vision for the charity.

Unless there has been an unusual infusion of cash by the founder, most nonprofits at this early stage face daunting financial challenges. In an effort to overcome those challenges, it is critical that the emerging organization establish a solid foundation of supporters who share a commitment to its mission and are willing to back that commitment with a financial investment.

Many organizations in this initial stage are struggling so hard for survival and to "get the message out" that they do not spend the requisite amount of time developing a detailed and actionable strategic plan that will lead the organization through its next several years.

At this stage, the organization presumably has defined or is developing some new and better way of providing a service or program to a population whose need is not being adequately met. This is where tremendous opportunity exists for the charitable investor who is seeking to have an impact through support of an innovative initiative.

To get involved with an emerging grass roots organization can be tremendously gratifying for a donor as you are "getting in on the ground floor" in support of a program or service that might have a profound influence on the community.

The risk in supporting an organization at this stage of development is that the group might not evolve past this stage. It might not develop a strong governing board, a sound leadership and staff, a solid corps of volunteers, clients or constituents, or most importantly, the broad base of financial resources necessary to sustaining the emerging agency in those first two years.

Philanthropists seeking to support an emerging organization with an innovative program can minimize the risk to their investment and help ensure its long-term return by doing the following:

- Examine the organization's written strategic plan to determine whether it is realistic and reliable, and whether it will lead to achieving the charity's stated vision

- Carefully study the written program or service outlines to insure that they make sense, and to determine whether a strong ongoing and follow-up evaluation component is built into program activities

- Review the credentials of the individuals and professionals who established the non-profit and who designed the program or service which you will support – do they have the experience and expertise to undertake a new enterprise?

- Determine whether the group is open and eager to draw additional supporters and experts into the ranks – they will have to be successful fundraisers and "friend raisers" if the organization is to thrive

- In addition to funding the actual program, service, or operating overhead of the organization, insist that a portion of the funds you provide be utilized for leadership training, technical assistance, and fund development training for the key people associated with the charity

- Lastly, don't walk away from your investment – stay in touch with the organization and its leadership to ensure that they are following the strategic plan and are implementing sound fund development and financial plans for the long-term health of the organization

Should your charitable gift to an emerging or grass roots organization pay off, the rewards can be enormous. In addition to providing programs and services in an innovative fashion to a populace in need, you have supported the establishment of a working model that can be replicated in other communities both far and near, thereby multiplying many times over the value of your initial charitable investment .

THE STAGE OF "MATURITY"

The second stage of development in the life of a nonprofit can be called the "maturing" stage. This stage is characterized by the following:

- The organization has survived infancy ("the terrible twos") and is getting stronger every day.

- The organization has recognized the need for an expanded, more diverse, more professional, and more knowledgeable board of directors. These individuals understand that they are charged with overseeing the health of the organization at present, as well as charting its course for the future, and for securing the resources necessary to navigating that course.

- There is now a paid management team, which includes specialists in the administrative functions, as well as experts in program and service areas, who are responsible for the day-to-day operations of the nonprofit.

- The mission and image of the charity are fairly well established. The emphasis is on ensuring that the organization's message is consistent and highly visible, as opposed to re-crafting it.

- Financially, the mature organization is operating on an even keel, always looking for new supporters and sources of funding, while recognizing the importance of maintaining the allegiance of existing donors.

At this stage of organizational development, the risk to your charitable investment – relative to return – is at its lowest. Programs and services are, theoretically, running smoothly, they have a proven track record, and they are serving an appropriate number of people relative to the size of the organization's annual operating budget.

In fact, it may seem like a "boring" investment. However, in this stage of its development, an organization can find it extremely difficult to secure ongoing support for successful initiatives. It seems like a paradox – when things are going well, it's almost more difficult to find donors who will invest in an ongoing program.

The reason for this is simple. Many charitable investors are always looking for what's new, what's exciting, what's innovative. The ongoing program starts to look like the "meat loaf" course on a buffet of great variety. Therefore, the philanthropist looking to make a very safe investment – one whose return can be fairly well predicted – can accomplish a great deal risking very little by looking to support an organization that is in this stage of its development.

Where is the risk in a "maintenance" phase organization? The risk lies in the possibility that the leadership will fall into complacency because things are running so smoothly. With things going well, trustees may become less active in pursuing new supporters. Donations level off as a result. New clients cannot receive services because funding is slipping even as the costs of providing them are rising. Meanwhile, volunteers, donors, and the community at large are looking for the next exciting program coming down the pike.

The biggest risk to the philanthropist donating to a maturing organization arises when the charity fails to assess or acknowledge changes in the environment in which they serve. Such changes might include a shifting demographic (e.g. the ethnic or cultural mix in the community); upturns or downturns in the economy; a change in the funding stream; advances in the organization's field of service (e.g. breakthroughs in medical research); or encouraging results from new or more innovative methodologies.

Another way to explain the notion of "changes in the environment" is by illustration. The eradication of polio was a dramatic alternation to the environment in which the March of Dimes came into existence. The March of Dimes shifted its focus in order to accommodate the changed medical research and support needs of that time.

A more contemporary example is the changing environment in which AIDS-focused charities function. Not many years ago, the mission of direct service organizations was to provide support for a dying constituency and their loved ones. With the advances in AIDS treatment, service organizations are now shifting their focus to providing assistance with the care and management of individuals who can and will live for many years despite carrying the AIDS virus. Thus, a significant shift in the medical treatment of AIDS necessitated charities that focused in that area to adjust both mission and programming in order to stay responsive to the changed needs of their service population. With the advances in AIDS treatment, however, came a change in the public's perception of the seriousness of the epidemic. In some communities, that change in perception has negatively affected funding for AIDS-focused charities.

Effective organizations in the field of AIDS-related services have had to remain flexible and responsive to these "changes in the environment" in order to remain both financially and functionally viable.

Philanthropists contributing to a mature organization can insure their investment by insisting on and supporting ongoing professional development on the part of the organization's leadership – board and staff—as well as encouraging and funding access to information which may have a bearing on the future course of the organization.

The biggest concern for you as a donor supporting an organization at this stage of development should be that the good work being accomplished as a result of your contribution will cease when your funding ceases; the organization's leadership has not planned nor made provisions for its future funding stream.

Ask to see the charity's strategic plan as a means of assessing its preparedness for the future.

THE RENEWAL/REVITALIZATION STAGE

The third significant stage in the life of a charitable organization is the phase of "renewal" or revitalization. This is the stage through which the organization transforms itself in response to environmental factors (or market forces) to insure that it continues to be as responsive as possible to the needs of its service population. Typical of this stage:

- The organization is undergoing a substantial degree of change: its programs and services are being updated, revamped, or, in some cases perhaps, being eliminated.

- New programs and services are being developed and implemented to meet the changing needs of the service population.

- The mission of the organization may change somewhat to more accurately reflect the agency's response to the changing needs of the service population.

- The organization is undertaking a revitalized effort to establish its image, its visibility, and its mission before the community in order to attract volunteers from segments of the community that have not yet been tapped, to attract clients for its programs and services, and most importantly, to attract new and expanded funding sources.

In some fashion, this stage of an organization's development is not completely unlike the emerging or grass roots stage in that it is marked by intense innovation and a moderate to high degree of organizational risk.

This, too, is an extremely exciting time for the philanthropic investor to get involved with an organization. On the one hand, the organization has been in existence for some period of years, thereby insuring that the charitable investment is not a totally risky one.

On the other hand, it is an opportunity for the philanthropic investor to get involved in innovative programs and services leading to new solutions, and to participate in the revitalization of the charity's mission.

To insure one's charitable investment at this phase of an organization's development, the philanthropist should encourage the charity to engage in safe and sound risk, as well as productive change. At the same time, be sure that the charity is not simply engaging in change for the sake of change. In other words, the philanthropist should keep a close eye on the motives underlying a changing dynamic within an organization or program. If innovation is the result of a clear assessment of alterations in the environment, this will bode well for the organization. If however, dramatic change is an impulsive act meant to "shock" the organization out of a slump, the charitable investor would do well to withhold financial support at this time.

STARTING ALL OVER AGAIN

"Force never moves in a straight line,
but always in a curve vast as the universe,
and therefore eventually returns whence it issued forth,
but upon a higher arc,
for the universe has progressed since it started."
— The Kabbalah

An organization that has successfully navigated the stage of renewal or revitalization in response to a changing environment will enter once again into a stage of maturity. During this phase, the changes and innovations that were initiated during the renewal stage in the areas of service, governance and administration will need to be integrated, stabilized, evaluated, and consolidated – always with one eye on the continually changing environment.

In fact a successful and healthy organization will alternate between periods of renewal/revitalization and maturity/stabilization.

To visualize the lifecycles of a nonprofit organization, imagine a "Slinky" toy gently stretched out. Organizations move through a continuous cyclical pattern of innovation and consolidation (renewal and stabilization) – never coming back to the same place twice, but always moving forward.

WHEN THE "SLINKY" COMES UNCOILED

There are two additional "mini"-stages in the lifecycle of a charitable organization. The healthiest of organizations will skim or skip through these phases without taking a lengthy, or costly, detour. These mini-phases are also known as "transition" points.

Transitions occur at the point where a mature organization – recognizing its need to adapt – begins the process of renewal. Conversely, another transition occurs as the organization begins to stabilize or consolidate the innovations it has adopted during the renewal stage.

By not responding quickly enough to changes in the environment – particularly the funding environment – organizations can slip into a kind of "free fall": funding plummets, the participation and enthusiasm of volunteers wanes, the leadership grows tired and frustrated, and management is operating on after-burner.

A charity slipping into "free fall" is not unlike a ship springing a leak – unless the leak is found and plugged quickly and effectively, the damage to the ship will increase. The longer an organization takes to recognize that it has bypassed a critical transition point without making appropriate adjustments, the longer it will take and the more resources it will consume to pull the organization back into a healthy lifecycle pattern.

Therefore, it is vitally important for the philanthropist to beware of investing heavily in an organization that has not recognized or responded to the fact that the world in which it operates has changed. Charitable investors are strongly urged to carefully examine an organization's written strategic plan before contributing heavily to a charity. Is the organization cognizant and prepared for what is up ahead, and has it developed a plan for successfully traveling through the anticipated changes?

CONFRONTING CRISIS

The other "mini"-stage, the phase one hopes no organization ever experiences, is that of "crisis." Crisis can occur at any time during an organization's lifecycle, and can take several forms:

- Crisis of leadership (for example, the untimely or unexpected death, resignation, or termination of one of the charity's key leaders)

- Operational crisis (for example, gross mismanagement of the organization's resources or the lodging of a lawsuit against the nonprofit, draining it financially)

- Crisis in the environment (for example, a change in the economy that substantially impacts the organization's funding stream such as a drop in the stock market in communities where substantial donor support comprised transfers of appreciated investments)

The philanthropist should be very careful about investing during a period of crisis. Chapter 6 will address how and when to consider providing emergency funding so that it will pose the lowest risk for your charitable investment.

SIZE AS RISK FACTOR

In assessing one's comfort level with a charity's organizational culture, as well as in determining the level of philanthropic "risk" a donor/investor is willing to accept, an important factor to consider is the size of an organization.

The smaller organization allows for the possibility of a relatively modest philanthropic investment to have a significant impact. Small charities can also provide the greatest opportunity for a high level of personal recognition and community appreciation. And finally, in the smaller organization, the leadership generally encourages – or at least does not discourage – active involvement by major donors in an advisory capacity

In a mid-sized organization, the philanthropic donor can enjoy a higher degree of anonymity if one so chooses, and still achieve a relatively significant impact on the community through the support of this established organization. An organization of moderate size, however, will generally prefer not to involve the donor in key organizational or programmatic decisions unless the donor also serves on the board of directors.

Large organizations, by virtue of their size, show evidence of having a successful organizational track record. For that reason, making a contribution to a large organization is very comfortable for many donors – they have a sense that their charitable investment is at very low risk. After all, in order to have become a large organization, the charity needed to have convinced many donors and other supporters that its operation is sound, its efforts are worthwhile, and that the agency is here to stay for the long term. This makes for a comfortable place where charitable investors can donate their funds.

Another low-risk charitable investment opportunity can be found in organizations having a dual national/local chapter structure. In some ways this may represent the soundest opportunity for a charitable investor.

On one hand, because contributions can be directed for use in the local community, donors are able to keep an eye on their investment and observe the tangible results of their gift. At the same time, the donor has a sense of assurance that the local chapter is operating to certain standards of sound management, leadership, and decision making because of the oversight provided by the national umbrella organization.

Do not accept this assumption at face value. This is not always the case. Donors would be well-advised to investigate the exact relationship between a local chapter and national umbrella organization when considering making a gift to such a charity.

When giving at the national level, the donor may feel less connected to the organization to which they are contributing. But if chosen carefully, a national organization may bear the greatest fruit when it comes to effecting policy or system change. If that is the "sphere of influence" you have selected for your philanthropic investments, nationally- or regionally-based organizations will have the greatest impact.

Finally, there is the option of providing funding to an international organization. There are two basic alternatives for international giving. One can contribute to an organization that operates solely in a country other than the one in which the donor resides. Alternatively, a philanthropist can invest in a domestically-based organization that operates across borders and in many countries (for example, the International Red Cross).

Because the laws and traditions governing the charitable sector in other countries may vary widely from the standards that have been set in the donor's home country, it is important to thoroughly understand how one's contribution will be utilized and monitored by an international organization. This is why many contributions made to specific foreign nations are made primarily through faith-based institutions (e.g. churches or religious groups). Donors generally feel more secure when channeling their support through an organization with which they are already comfortable or familiar.

ORGANIZATIONAL BUDGET AS A RISK INDICATOR

Another means for assessing the level of philanthropic risk represented by your choice of charity is to look at the organization's budget. Because of continuing financial scandals being uncovered in major national organizations in the United States, donors have begun to realize that there may be some distinct advantages to making their charitable investments in organizations of very modest means.

For example, if an organization is capable of performing a tremendous service in the community, affecting a large number of people, using innovative means and methods, and is doing so with an annual operating budget under a $100,000, it is highly unlikely that there is a lot of "slack" in the budget or a mismanagement of funds. A charitable investment of virtually any size in an organization with that profile can have quite a dramatic impact on the community, as well as on the organization's ability to build support from other funders.

That is not to say that organizations that are operating with significantly higher budgets – whether it is $2 million, $5 million, $20 million, or a hundred million dollars – are less effective or are more wasteful. It may be true, however, that organizations that are relatively "well off" compared to the rest of the nonprofit sector may be a little less cost conscious in their approach to solving society's problems.

In fact, one of the key problems we see in the largest organizations in the charitable sector is the same problem that we see in many of our largest businesses and corporations. Innovation and respect for human resources as an organization's most valuable assets are replaced by a misguided belief that the simple application of funds to a problem will solve that problem.

HOW IMPORTANT – REALLY – IS MONEY?

"Treating money as the problem
is like blaming the thermometer for your fever"
- Stephen Chapman

Ask most nonprofits operating today to name their single largest problem, and they will tell you that it is a lack of money. In the charitable sector, however, lack of money is rarely the real problem. The money problem is only a symptom.

Organizations with outstanding leadership, sound management, a strong mission, effective programs and services reflective of that mission, and a welcoming attitude toward new constituents (donors, volunteers, and clients alike) do not suffer money problems. It is when one of those key elements is out of sync that an organization begins to feel the pain financially.

That is why a large and wealthy organization can often operate at less than optimum performance levels before realizing that there are internal organizational problems. Financial "comfort" can act as a mask – even to the leaders of an organization – obscuring very real problems of governance, administration or service until well past a point where the problem would be simple to address.

For that reason, the larger the gift to the wealthier the organization, the more critical it becomes for a philanthropic investor to have specific knowledge about the way in which that investment will be applied. As a donor, you want to ensure that your contribution will not serve as a temporary patch on a tire that's fundamentally shot, only to let the organization wobble down the road a little further.

SUMMARY

Just as in financial investing, a philanthropic investor should come to terms with the level of investment risk with which they will feel comfortable – before committing to a major contribution. The "risk" factor in the charitable environment can be assessed by examining the organization's overall operational size, its budget and the stage of development in which it finds itself.

In terms of organizational lifecycles, the charity that is in the emerging stage or in the renewal/revitalization stage embodies the highest level of risk for the philanthropic investor. In many instances, however, those charities provide opportunity for the greatest social return on investment.

An organization in the maturing stage offers a sound, lower risk investment for the philanthropist. The charitable investor should take great care when considering a contribution to an organization that is either in transition or in crisis.

CHAPTER 6

HOW WILL YOUR MONEY BE USED?

"When you write the checks,
you get the power to change things."
— Jeffrey D. Jacobs

T O PLACE YOUR CHARITABLE INVESTMENT MOST EFFECTIVELY, your funds should be targeted for a specific kind of use by the organization you have selected as the beneficiary.

ALL MONEY IS NOT THE SAME

There are essentially eight types of funding which a charity needs in order to fulfill its mission and deliver its programs and services while insuring the long-term fiscal stability of its operation.

CAPITAL SUPPORT

This is funding that an organization seeks in order to build a new facility, expand its current facility, or purchase major equipment, land or buildings. An organization will typically seek the largest gifts first, eventually working its way down through progressively lower levels of giving, until it has achieved its overall capital campaign goal. Frequently, those donors making the largest gifts, known as "lead gifts," are offered an opportunity to have the building, or a section of the building, named in their honor.

Many donors find capital funding a highly gratifying form of philan-thropy for two reasons. First, the donor can be confident that the support provided is being used in a tangible and necessary fashion as evidenced by the actual construction of the facility or the purchase of equipment. Second-ly, donors seeking long-term and highly visible recognition can ensure that their memory, or that of the person they choose to honor, will remain visible for a long, long time.

In the right setting, the building or facility may even become synony-mous with the donor's name, as in the case of institutions such as the Norris Cancer Research Center, the Dorothy Chandler Pavilion, the Annenberg Center for Health Sciences, or the Getty Museum.

ENDOWMENT FUNDS

Endowment monies are funds that are invested in order to provide future, long-term support for the organization. Providing endowment funding is a charitable "investment" in the most real sense, for the return is both long-term and ongoing. In essence, endowment funds generate interest revenue on an annual basis, which the nonprofit may choose to utilize in a number of fashions. For example, a portion of the annual endowment revenue may be used to cover the charity's operating or overhead expenses. Or, those funds might be utilized to initiate or expand programs and services. The revenue can also be used for capital renovations, or extraordinary organizational needs. Most often, smaller- and mid-sized organizations (for those few that actually have an endowment) invest the generated proceeds back into the endowment, thereby growing its principal.

Endowment funding can be provided on an unrestricted basis. That is, the donor allows the charity to choose how it will utilize the endowment and the revenue generated by it. This decision is one most appropriately made by the board of directors or trustees. Or, a donor may choose to restrict the use of the funding that he or she provides for an endowment to a specific purpose. For example, to "endow a chair" at a university is to provide funding that will generate revenue to meet or subsidize the salary requirements for that particular faculty position. Alternatively, one can endow a program or specific project in order to ensure that there will be an ongoing stream of revenue to maintain that program for the long term.

In some cases it is possible to request or negotiate the naming of a building, wing, or program, in recognition for a substantial endowment gift, even if that endowment is not specifically related to the naming opportunity.

GENERAL OPERATING SUPPORT

Operating funds are those that are needed to cover the daily costs involved in running a charity and its programs. Operating monies cover those expenses that, although necessary, are not specifically or directly related to a program or service. For example, an organization that provides volunteer assistance to local schools may have only limited expenses directly related to that service. However, the organization maintains the central office from which staff members solicit and assign volunteers. Their overhead costs may include rent, telephone expenses, postage, photocopying, electricity, heating and air conditioning, paper clips, rubber bands, basic furniture, and a computer. The chair, the desk, and the paper clips are not technically program-specific expenses, but the organization couldn't do business without them.

It is very difficult for organizations to raise general operating funds. Donors, both individuals and foundations, are reluctant to provide funding that does not have an immediate and visible impact on the population they wish to benefit. As a result, many very fine nonprofit agencies may be adequately funded for their programs and services, but are struggling to survive because of the difficulty in securing funds to meet their overhead expenses.

A philanthropist considering making a gift of general operating funds can maximize that investment by guaranteeing operational support for a multi-year period. A one-year contribution may result in the organization facing the same lack of general operating support the following year and the donor realizing virtually no return on his or her investment. In tandem with providing longer-term operating support, the charitable investor should encourage, and perhaps require, that organizations receive technical assistance and training to help diversify their fundraising activities such that they will be able to maintain the necessary level of operational support in the years to come.

SEED MONEY/PILOT MONEY

This is money that an organization needs in order to undertake a new project or service, or in some cases to start up an entirely new nonprofit. Clearly a gift of seed or pilot money is a high-risk investment – there is no track record that the philanthropist can review in order to determine whether the organization is likely to be successful in its new endeavor.

On the other hand, the philanthropist has the opportunity to get in on the "ground floor" of what may be an extremely dynamic and high effective initiative.

With seed or pilot money, it is absolutely critical – perhaps more so than with any other type of funding – to investigate the leadership, fiscal stability, program methodology, evaluation plans, and other sources of support before making an investment decision.

PROGRAM FUNDS

These are funds that are used in order to finance an ongoing program or service. Ideally, this funding will be used to expand program capabilities or reach, to increase the number of persons benefiting from an existing initiative, or to improve the overall quality of an already existing service.

Providing ongoing program funds is a very low-risk proposition. Presumably there is a track record of success showing a charitable investor that the application of their funds to the program will achieve the results the donors have specified. Further, ongoing programs generally have multiple sources of support, which means that other charitable investors have evaluated this organization and program and determined it to be worthy.

Although a safe investment, donors may not see as significant an impact on the community as they might through the funding of a new initiative.

Recognition may be another factor to consider. Unless the level of financial support for a program is extraordinary, or is committed over a long period of time, recognition of the donor's gift may be somewhat modest.

MATCHING/CHALLENGE FUNDS

This is funding that the philanthropist provides for use by the organization as its "magnet" money. In otherwords, the donor is providing a contribution to the organization not only to serve the organization's needs relative to operational costs, capital costs, or program costs, but is also giving the organization use of the money for the purpose of attracting other investors.

How does this work? As a donor who may be interested in supporting, for example, local literacy programs, it is not unlikely that three or four organizations might approach you with a request for funds. All things being equal – that is, the fiscal stability of the organization, the quality and commitment of its leadership, the successful track record of the program, and a solid base of support in the community – the wise investor will make his or her charitable contribution to that organization where the investment might be worth literally double its value. Most organizations will be able to promise only that "if you give us one dollar, we will provide one dollar's worth of service to the community." However, the charity with a matching grant from another donor can make the statement that "if you give us one dollar, it will be matched by one dollar from another donor who has given us a special grant for this purpose. Therefore, with your one-dollar contribution, we will be able to provide two dollars' worth of service to the community." By structuring your gift as a challenge or matching gift, you as a donor can double the value of your investment.

There is a slight difference between a matching fund and a challenge fund, although the two terms are often used interchangeably. In a matching situation, the donor agrees that for each dollar raised, up to specified limits, the donor will "match" that gift at some ratio. For example, with a 1:1 ratio, for each dollar raised by the organization, the donor will provide one dollar. Therefore, if the donor provides a matching grant in the amount of $10,000, with a 1:1 matching ratio, the donor will have to provide funding equal to the amount raised by the charity from other sources up to that $10,000 limit. In a matching grant situation if the organization is able to raise only $9,999, the donor matches with $9,999.

With a challenge grant, the donor specifies a target amount which the organization must raise before the donor will provide corresponding funds on the basis of some ratio. For example, the donor may issue a challenge grant of $10,000, with a 1:1 ratio. When, and only when, the organization raises $10,000 from other sources, will the donor provide his or her grant of $10,000. In a challenge situation, if the charity raises only $9,999, the donor can choose to give nothing, as the charity has not met the challenge.

Matching and challenge funding is very exciting for the philanthropic investor. First of all, it is a very low-risk investment. To enter into a matching or challenge arrangement, a charity must be confident that its programs and services are so strong that they will be attractive to other founders. The charity must also be confident that it is proficient enough in its fundraising methodologies that it will raise as much money as is necessary in order to meet the matching target or the challenge goal.

Just as the other donors whose funds will be solicited to meet your match will have doubled their investment value, so, too, will your contribution be doubled in value. Further, by requiring that an organization stretch its abilities and capabilities in the fund development arena, the philanthropist is strengthening the infrastructure of that charity such that its long-term health and success are insured. Thus, the matching or challenge grant provides a variety of returns for the charitable investor.

EMERGENCY FUNDS

Undoubtedly, this is a very risky form of charitable investment. There can be only two types of emergencies that an organization might face in its lifetime. One is an emergency initiated by a force outside of the control or influence of the charitable entity. For example, a hurricane, tornado, or earthquake destroys an organization's facility. Clearly, the charity had no way of foreseeing that this might happen, and probably is not in a financial position to address an emergency of that magnitude out of its general funds.

In such case, a charitable gift of emergency funding can have a double effect. First, there is the immediate impact that the emergency funds will have on the lives of the people served by the endangered organization: the hungry, homeless, the battered, students, the ill, etc. Moreover, when natural disaster strikes, programs and services already operating at full capacity tend to become strained by the additional number of community members who have also been affected by these catastrophic circumstances.

Without emergency funding, disaster can also spell the end for an effective and much-needed charity. Shutting down due to catastrophe is like watching the railroad tracks simply end.

A gift of emergency funding not only impacts the lives of individuals in the community at that moment, but it can ensure the ongoing existence of a charitable organization so that it can continue to serve for years and generations to come.

Beware, however, the other category of "emergency." This is the emergency that is wholly man-made in nature and generally manifests itself as an announcement that the doors will close next week (or next month) because the charity has run out of cash. This type of emergency is no emergency at all. It is simply proof that someone at the charity "fell asleep at the switch." And that "someone," almost without fail, is the board of the organization. No charity comes that near to its doors being closed without red flags appearing at least six to eight months in advance of the emergency. Those signs would have been evident in the organization's financial statements, staff morale, word of mouth in the community, and a host of other means that would be difficult to ignore.

To invest emergency funds in an organization suffering from a man-made emergency is to risk throwing good money after bad. Only in very rare circumstances should a philanthropist consider making a substantial gift to an organization that has clearly mismanaged its resources prior to this point.

These circumstances would include situations in which the failure or shutdown of the organization would severely impair the well-being or quality of life for a major segment of the community's population. Further, the longer the charity has been in existence, the more likely it is that the organization will be able to muster the internal resources – as well as the broad base of community support – that it will need if it is to be helped over this hump.

Lastly and most importantly, it is absolutely critical that before any emergency funding is committed, the board of directors or some subset of that group must detail an actionable strategic plan that is designed to not only pull the charity from the brink of disaster, but to ensure the establishment of a solid foundation for ongoing long-term success.

From experience, we can tell you that in a man-made emergency, rarely will one find the unique set of circumstances that would warrant a philanthropic infusion of funding. Just as a giraffe is not able to change its spots, so, too, is it difficult for a group of trustees to change the patterns, thinking, and decision-making habits that led to imminent disaster.

LOANS/INVESTMENTS

In this complex form of charitable giving, the philanthropist may choose to support an organization or project in which traditional financial institutions would be unwilling to invest, or for which they would charge interest rates prohibitive for a charity. Although this type of funding is not initially structured as an outright gift, the donor may choose to convert it to such at any point he or she desires.

For example, a highly successful, fast growing, and much needed charity may be in desperate need to expand its facility as quickly as possible. Delaying construction until the funding can be raised through a traditional capital campaign may create an unacceptable burden on the client population. In such a situation, a charity may seek to borrow funding so that construction can commence even while contributions are being sought. Commercial lenders, if even interested in lending money to a charity, will most likely have to charge competitive market rates, which would be prohibitive for most nonprofit organizations.

In such an instance, the philanthropist could offer to provide the much-needed support to the charity in the form of a low-interest loan. Clearly, the donor would want to perform due diligence on the organization, its leaders, and its financial history. If all is in order, the charitable investor can have both a major impact on the community through his or her gift of support, as well as get back that funding to use for assisting that same or another organization.

Clearly, there is some risk involved here. The organization, feeling "secure" because of the loan, may not be as aggressive as it otherwise would be in pursuing contributed funds. Further, should the fortunes of the organization change over time such that it is unable to meet debt service, the philanthropist will be in the awkward position of deciding how and at what level of intensity to pursue remuneration.

Therefore, it is critical that the charitable investor and the leadership of the nonprofit organization are clear and candid with one another with respect to terms, conditions, expected communications, and consequences relative to repayment...and that they put it in writing!

SUMMARY

Direct financial support to a charitable organization can take a variety of different forms. Some of these offer a lower or higher risk factor, as well as varying rates of "philanthropic return." Some forms of support are more appropriate in the context of a short-term relationship with the organization. Other forms are sensible charitable investments only when conceived of as a long-term, ongoing relationship with the selected agency.

In either case, you must make your decision true to your own long-term vision for a better world, stronger community, or heightened quality of life for your fellow man.

PART THREE

INVESTIGATING OPPORTUNITES FOR YOUR CHARITABLE INVESTMENT

CHAPTER 7

FINDING A CHARITY
THAT SHARES YOUR GOALS

*"Human beings, who are almost unique in having the
ability to learn from the experience of others, are also
remarkable for their apparent disinclination to do so."*

– Douglas Adams

OW DO YOU BEGIN TO LOOK FOR A CHARITABLE ORGANIZATION that shares your vision and your goals? The first step is to review the decisions you've already made following the guidelines set out in the previous chapters:

- Drawing on your personal history, in which field of service would you like to focus your philanthropy?

- What is the sphere of influence or desired level of impact you wish to have through your charitable giving: personal, community, institutional, or policy?

- Which is the community you have chosen to benefit through your contributions?

- Have you defined the level of "investment risk" with which you will feel most comfortable?

- With respect to budget, have you determined whether you would like your contribution to constitute a substantial portion of a smaller budget or operation? Or would you feel as comfortable starting with a small or moderate contribution to an organization of a size where your contribution might receive less recognition?

Once you have answered these questions as specifically as possible to your own and your family's satisfaction, only then can you start to identify and investigate organizations whose work and profiles most closely match your philanthropic investment objectives.

WHERE TO START

The best way to start is by speaking to other "investors." By this, we mean you should contact other individuals, organizations, or institutions that provide substantial funding to a broad range of nonprofits – or advise nonprofits – at least some of which may fall in the category that you would like to support.

COMMUNITY FOUNDATIONS

Community foundations are a great resource, and can be found across the country. In essence, community foundations are organized to benefit charities and people who live within a specified geographic area. For example, the California Community Foundation is organized to benefit nonprofits and communities throughout the state of California. The DuPage (IL) Community Foundation, on the other hand, is organized to benefit agencies only within that specific county. Many cities have their own community foundations.

Community foundations are themselves charities set up specifically to manage and distribute charitable funds that are generally also drawn from the geographic region that they benefit. Consequently, community foundations function as an objective resource for information on a broad range of agencies and organizations within the region that they encompass.

Community foundations receive numerous proposals for support from organizations within their community. Part of the foundation's function is to evaluate not only those proposals, but also the organizations that have submitted them. As a result, community foundations have their finger on the pulse of the nonprofit sector within that specified region, and can be a wonderful source for information on who is doing what, who is doing it well, and who is in need and deserving of support.

Further, the community foundation may have specific information about a given organization in that community that may help you to determine whether or not to consider a contribution to or investment in that particular charity.

A community foundation may also be able to let you know whether there is an existing nonprofit, project, or initiative that matches the profile of the work you would like to support.

Or, perhaps you have identified an unmet need in your chosen community. The community foundation can be a wonderful resource to help you determine whether and how to launch your own charitable initiative.

GRANT-MAKING ORGANIZATIONS

Another source of information on charitable groups that meet your investment goals are other grant-making organizations. Most frequently, these organizations are private, independent foundations sponsored by individuals or families who are seriously involved in charitable giving.

The most prominent alliance of such foundations is the Council on Foundations. The Council is a membership organization of foundations found across the country that are organized into smaller, regional entities known as Regional Associations of Grantmakers (RAGs). For example, one prominent RAG is the Donors Forum of Chicago.

Contact a local regional association of grantmakers and let them know about your particular charitable giving interests. They can direct you to member foundations that fund similar activities.

You can contact these and other foundations that fund or support activities or projects of the type in which you are interested, and thus start developing your own list of prospects.

MANAGEMENT SUPPORT ORGANIZATIONS (A/K/A TECHNICAL ASSISTANCE CENTERS)

Another excellent resource for information on organizations and initiatives are the many management support organizations (MSOs) located throughout the country. These are generally nonprofit organizations whose mission is to provide education, consultation, training, and other resources to nonprofit organizations. MSOs interface with large numbers of charities on a regular, often daily, basis. They operate very closely with the nonprofit community, and therefore are often the most knowledgeable source about a local community's nonprofit sector, about changing or unmet needs within a particular community, and about the effectiveness of specific organizations.

Technical assistance agencies (another name for MSOs) can take many forms. In some communities the Volunteer Center is the major resource for nonprofits. In other communities it may be known as the Support Center. The network of technical assistance providers includes a wide range of organizations, many of whom belong to or are members of the Nonprofit Management Association.

The local United Way chapter in the community which you would like to benefit may be a source of information about organizations doing work of the type you are interested in funding. At the very least, the United Way should be able to direct you to the nearest community foundation, Regional Association of Grantmakers, or technical assistance provider.

EXPERTS

Another wonderful source of leads are "experts in the field." These may be academic professionals, consultants, or practitioners in the field, who are highly knowledgeable about those organizations and institutions that are engaged in cutting-edge, exemplary, or highly effective work. Check with universities located in the area you wish to benefit to see whether they have a degree or certificate program in philanthropy or nonprofit management. Contact their faculty and lecturers for recommendations on charities matching your interest profile.

HOW TO USE THESE RESOURCES

More important than what you ask will be what you tell them. First, be sure that you are talking to the right person. Generally the "right person" will be the executive director, and once the switchboard operator understands that you are a potential donor looking for assistance, there should be no problem in having your call put through to the appropriate party.

Let your contact know specifically what kinds of initiatives you would like to support through your charitable contributions. Include all the information that was reviewed earlier: the field of service, sphere of influence, community, organization size and budget. The more specific you can be about your parameters, the more helpful they can be with suggestions or recommendations.

Ask if they know of any organizations whose work matches the profile you have described. Be sure that in their recommendation they include organizations that they have not been able to fund as well as organizations which they themselves have supported.

It is not unusual for a foundation to receive many more applications for funding than they can possibly accommodate. As a result, many fine nonprofits end up on the "declined" pile simply because the funder ran out of grant money.

In other cases, the foundation has set its guidelines very specifically, and numerous nonprofits doing very fine work have their requests for funding rejected because their activities fall outside of the granting institution's current field of interest.

Do not look to these contacts for specific references, recommendations or opinions on whether or not you should support any given organization. Rather, look to these sources to help you in compiling a list of charities to investigate yourself, or to have investigated on your behalf.

Again, the key to putting together a strong list of candidates for your charitable investment is knowing precisely what it is you would like to accomplish with your philanthropic giving.

WHEN THERE IS NO MATCH

There are two routes you can follow should you find that there really are no charities doing the kind of work you would like to fund.

The simplest solution is to simply look harder. You may find that the kind of organization doing the work you wish to support falls into a "crack" such that it will not appear on the radar screen of the community foundation, a private foundation, a technical assistance center, or organizations such as the United Way.

In that case, one of the most effective ways to find those organizations is to "advertise." This is not to suggest that you should advertise in a general publication. However, there are a number of trade and professional journals and publications – both in print and now on-line – which serve the non-profit sector. Nonprofits serious about their work regularly read or review these major informational resources. These might include the *Chronicle of Philanthropy, Non Profit Times,* and *Contributions,* as well as a variety of other charitable sector publications. Additionally, technical assistance providers, volunteer centers, and other such associations or alliances of non-profits have their own newsletters or member communication devices.

All of these will be happy to post your listing of funds that you may have available for a particular type of project or organization.

In your ad, be as specific as possible in defining the type of project and organization from which you would like to hear. Be sure to request that responses be directed to a post office box provided by the publication, to the consultant you may have assisting you, or to some other "blind" mail box. This will insure your privacy as well as screen you from the flood of responses such a notice can generate for some time to come.

WRITING THE AD

In your notice, define the parameters within which a prospective beneficiary organization must fall: program type, location, size, exact population served, etc. Request an initial letter of inquiry – no longer than two pages – in which the organization is to describe its project or activity, and how, exactly, it matches the profile which you have described in your advertisement.

Two pages provide ample space to provide critical information which would allow you to determine whether or not you wish to further investigate a charity. It also forces the organization to get right to the point about what they do, why it's valuable, and how it meets the criteria that you have stipulated.

Should any of the responding charities catch your interest, you should request further and more specific information from them. At this point, you would send them a more comprehensive description of your funding guidelines, as well as an in-depth application for them to complete (samples of both can be found at www.SmartGenerosity.com). Avoid accepting "free form" narrative proposals. First, they can be murderously boring to wade through – without ever getting to the information that is of most importance to you. Also, it is easier to hide negative information in a barrage of other positive "stuff."

GOING OFF THE BEATEN TRACK

"Two roads diverged in a wood,
and I...I took the one less traveled by,
and that has made all the difference."
– Robert Frost

It would seem that these methods and resources for finding nonprofit organizations are the most effective in larger communities or metro-politan areas, or when trying to uncover fairly sophisticated or "known" organizations. Where do you begin the search when you are for looking for an organization that is, quite literally, "off the beaten track"?

If the kind of charity you are looking for is off the beaten track, it will be known to, at the very least, the individuals who serve as the board directors and volunteers for that charity. In smaller or rural communities, these persons often hold leadership positions in other community-based entities. Members of the local Chamber of Commerce, Rotary, Soroptimists, Lions, Elks, faith congregations, and other associations of highly involved community members can be great resources for finding organizations that may have a very low profile.

One can also research the names of all of the tax-exempt charitable organizations within a given state or zip code on the Internal Revenue Service's web site. It lists any tax-exempt nonprofit that is required to file an annual informational tax return (Form 990). The IRS listings, however, provide only minimal information which may or may not be of use in making your charitable investment decision.

SUMMARY

Once you have defined the parameters for your charitable investments, it should not be difficult to find the names of and information about the organizations that match your investment profile.

The charitable community – and each of its sectors – is made up of generous individuals who will be happy to help you in your quest to find those organizations doing the type and quality of work that you are anxious to support.

CHAPTER 8

LOOK BEFORE YOU LEAP: PERFORMING DUE DILIGENCE

"I've known everyone on the board for years, and they're great people."

"They have a very inpressive website."

"I always see them in the paper. They must be a worthy cause."

"Well, it's a national charity that's been around forever...
by giving to them, I know where my money goes!"

B. UT, WHAT DO YOU REALLY KNOW?

- How many of us knew a few years back that the chief executive of the most prosperous and respected federated campaign organization in the nation was using substantial agency funds to further his relationships with various women – among other improper and illegal uses of our hard-earned contributions?

- Were the residents of one small community aware that nearly a quarter of their senior service agency's annual budget had been embezzled?

- Would you have invested several hundred thousand dollars of your funds in short-term CDs? You probably didn't know that one well-respected regional charity chose this strategy for growing their reserve because they just didn't know any better.

- And if you knew, would you care that numerous high-visibility galas across this country net less money for programs and service than the combined price of the flowers, decorations, and entertainment for those same events?

As a donor, in most cases, you only know what a nonprofit wants you to know. And for good reason – they want and need your money. Yet philanthropists are not nearly as diligent about investigating charities as they are about analyzing comparably-sized personal investment opportunities.

WHAT ELEMENTS COMPRISE DUE DILIGENCE OF A NONPROFIT?

There are four main areas that are critical to determining whether or not a nonprofit organization represents a sound "risk" for your charitable contribution:

A. MISSION AND PROGRAMS

The charity's leadership should be absolutely clear about the essential nature of the organization's work, and how each and every program and service of the nonprofit is directly related to that mission.

The healthy organization will be concise and specific in addressing the following mission-related questions:

1. Who are we? Who comprises the organization?

2. Who do we seek to serve?

3. In what geographical area or communities do we provide our programs and services?

4. What vital, critical, urgent human need do we seek to address?

5. How do we serve this need differently than any other organization seeking to address this same issue?

6. In essence, what change in the world do we seek to make?

7. Why are we deserving of a donor's money?

Those charities that have a strong focus, a serious sense of purpose, and an overview of the "the big picture" will have no problem giving you a succinct answer to these questions. That's because the answers to these questions inform their daily work.

If an organization finds it simpler to "laundry list" its programs and services than to communicate an overarching mission, you may wish to take pause before making a substantial contribution there.

B. PROGRAMS AND SERVICES

With respect to programs and services, it is important to determine whether those activities are truly reflective of the values and priorities addressed in the overall mission of the organization. Programs and services do not equal mission. Rather, programs and services should be an expression of the overall mission in action. In gauging the strength of a charity's actual work, a prospective donor should ask these key program-related questions.

1. Does the organization seem to jump onto whatever "bandwagon" of service is popular with the public (or attractive to funders) at any given time without really connecting it to the mission or existing programs? This would indicate that resources are being applied to activities primarily on the basis of what's "fashionable" rather than what's effective or needed.

2. Does each program and service address a specific issue or need?

3. Does it address that need in a way that is effective and measurable?

4. Does the organization maintain an ongoing process of evaluation to assess whether its programs and services are in fact achieving the desired or intended results?

5. Do the programs and services consume a disproportionately small percentage of the nonprofit's resources relative to the expenditures being made for overhead, fund raising events, and other "special" activities? In the strongest and most successful organizations, service will always be the priority.

In general, weak organizations are those with a very broad or unfocused mission, where programs seem to relate neither to the mission nor to the organization's other activities.

C. QUALITY AND COMMITMENT OF THE LEADERSHIP OF THE ORGANIZATION

This factor, more than any other, is underutilized as a major indicator of whether an organization is capable of and committed to achieving the objectives intended through your contribution.

By "leadership of the organization," we are referring to those individuals who hold the ultimate authority, the greatest responsibility, and the fiduciary obligation for a non-profit corporation: that leadership is the board of directors or board of trustees.

The executive director and the senior administrative staff members are all critical players. However, they are paid employees who function under the guidance and direction of the board. The board has – or should have – the ultimate power and control over the organization.

The quality of the board can and should be measured in several different ways:

1. Is the board of directors large enough to encompass the many types of expertise and representation that would be necessary for guiding a organization with this mission and this size budget? At the same time, is the board small enough that each director feels a compelling personal responsibility for the sound and ethical governance of the institution?

2. Does the board, in fact, have represented among its members professionals or experts knowledgeable in key areas such as finance, law, fund raising, and business management, as well as professionals and experts from the field or fields of the organization's primary endeavor? For example, does the board of an educational institution have any educators on the board? Does an arts-oriented charity

have a practicing artist on the board? Are individual board members actively engaged in committee work related to the functional or operational areas in which they have expertise?

3. Does the board have members to act as both representatives and "ambassadors" to the many sectors of the community that the organization seeks to either serve or solicit? Do board members hold positions of visibility or authority elsewhere in the community such that their personal or professional stature enhances the image and reputation of the nonprofit?

4. Do board members take an active role in establishing policy, the strategic plan, and a long-term vision for the organization?

Evaluating the commitment of the leadership is another matter:

1. Do all members of the board of directors or trustees meet on a regular and consistent basis appropriate to the scope, level, budget and nature of work required to successfully direct an organization of its size?

2. When meeting as a board, do these "stewards" of the organization focus their attention and discussions on those matters requiring policy-level attention, or do they spend their time together discussing matters more appropriate to the staff?

3. Does each board member have a clear understanding of the specific reason he or she was asked to serve on the board, and what his or her unique role on the board is at this time? Is that understanding reflected in each board member's assignment to and participation in committee work?

4. Has each board member made an annual financial contribution to the organization at a level reflective of the priority that organization's work holds in that director's life?

This issue of determining whether every board member contributes financially to the organization should be critical to your own donation decision.

Would you make a major investment in a company or venture in which the owners and founders had no stake? You would at least think twice before putting money into the firm, and you would probably maintain some level of oversight or control over that investment once it was made.

Yet every day, philanthropists and major donors make significant contributions to charities without verifying the "owners'" (i.e. board members') participation.

There is a good reason why many institutional funders – foundations and corporations – demand to know what percentage of directors on a given board contribute to that charity.

They know that a board managing its own contributions as well as those of the public will often be more deliberate in its financial and planning decisions. The internal standards of accountability are often higher when board members' own money is at stake.

What should be more telling to the discriminating donor, however, is the fact of whether board members give at all.

In a survey of one hundred nonprofits with annual budgets ranging from $100,000 to $4 million and with boards sized 3 to 30, less than 10% reported that each member of the board made a monetary gift beyond the purchase of an event ticket or some other exchange-for-value contribution.

The size of contribution is almost irrelevant – for some trustees, a donation of $10 might constitute a personal sacrifice, where for others a gift of $10,000 would be simple. A financial contribution is a tangible sign of a director's faith in the organization, its mission, its leadership and its direction.

Before making your charitable investment, inquire about the board's donation track record. Then decide if you would trust them to manage your money.

D. FINANCIAL STABILITY OF THE ORGANIZATION

Just as with any investment opportunity, when considering a substantial charitable contribution, it is critical that the philanthropist examine key

financial indicators for the organization:

1. Does the organization engage an independent, certified public accounting firm or professional on an annual basis to prepare audited financial statements? If not, does the organization have a compilation prepared by an accounting professional on an annual basis? Is there an independent audit committee?

2. Does the organization consistently establish and approve an annual operating budget prior to the beginning of each fiscal year? Is that budget tracked in relation to actual expenditures and income over the course of the year? Is a variance report prepared and distributed to each board member on a regular basis? Does each board member understand how to read and interpret the organization's financial documents? Are the financial documents used as decision-making tools or are they organizational "window dressing"?

3. Has the organization run in the black consistently for the last three years? If there has been a substantial surplus, how has the board of directors chosen to utilize those funds? If the organization is running a deficit, is this a first-time deficit, or has the organization been operating at a loss for an extended period of time? If this is a first-time deficit, is there a clear understanding or explanation on the part of the board for why and how this occurred? Has the board developed a written plan to insure that the deficit situation does not repeat itself in the coming fiscal year?

4. Does the organization maintain any type or types of reserve funds, such as a capital reserve, or an endowment fund? If so, who is responsible for overseeing or investing those funds in order to maximize their

value? Does the organization have a written and regularly-updated investment policy?

E. WHAT OTHER INDIVIDUALS OR ENTITIES HAVE INVESTED IN THIS ORGANIZATION?

If the organization has been successful in attracting financial support from other individuals whose judgment you respect, or from institutional funders such as foundations or corporations that have rigorous standards and requirements in order to qualify for funding, the "risk" to your investment diminishes. This is true also if the organization has successfully negotiated a loan process with a commercial lender.

The key questions relative to other investors include:

1. What other major donors or funders have undertaken a comprehensive assessment of this organization and have deemed it worthy of a substantial financial contribution?

2. Who can you contact to verify those funders' or donors' findings?

If you have been approached or are considering becoming an early contributor to a new organization or campaign, there may be very little "investor" history for you to reference. In that case, you must take special care in assessing the other three factors: mission, leadership and overall fiscal stability.

Now that you know what to evaluate in a due diligence process, how do you actually go about performing the due diligence? And how can you go about investigating a nonprofit that may be located geographically at some distance from you?

PERFORMING THE DUE DILIGENCE

You have one objective in performing the due diligence: to insure that the organization in which you are considering making a charitable investment is capable of and committed to using your investment as effectively as possible to accomplish your personal philanthropic objectives.

Again, the major factors you will be assessing are the agency's mission and programs; its financial stability; the quality and commitment of the organization's leadership; and the confidence level of its other "investors."

There are three methods for performing the due diligence. One method relies solely on an examination of key organizational documents. The other two methods combine comprehensive in-person and on-site examinations with document analysis.

METHOD ONE: DOCUMENT ANALYSIS
STEP 1: INITIAL TELEPHONE CONTACT

Contact the executive director of the organization about which you would like more information. Let them know that the agency is one of a number of organizations under consideration for a substantial charitable contribution. Ask that the group send you a letter, no more than two pages in length, providing essential information about the organization: what it does, who it serves, what social issue or problem it addresses, and how it does so in a fashion unique from other agencies.

Make note of the way in which you were handled on the telephone. Were all members of the staff with whom you spoke courteous, pleasant, and responsive? Was there a major change in how you were dealt with once your interest as a potential donor became known? If you were someone needing services from this agency, would you feel equally welcomed and comfortable in calling?

STEP 2: REVIEW OF LETTER RESPONSES

Set aside any letters indicating that the organization or its work do not match the focus you have selected for your philanthropic giving. You should send a brief courtesy note to such agencies, thanking them for their response and letting them know that at this point in time, you are unable to make a contribution. We often suggest sending a modest donation to those organizations as a means of showing your general support for their work, while making it clear that a larger contribution is not forthcoming at this time. (Surprisingly, some organizations have been so compelling in their appreciation for even this modest contribution that philanthropists reconsider their decision and do end up pursuing a longer-term and more generous relationship!)

For those organizations that have impressed you with their response and responsiveness to your inquiry – and whose profiles seems to match your personal philanthropic interest as determined earlier – it is time to submit a complete proposal.

STEP 3: REQUEST FOR PROPOSAL

Prepare a standard form letter to send to those organizations that seem a strong match for your funding interests, requesting that they submit a proposal consisting of the following items only:

- A brief overview of the organization's history and its mission

- A brief overview of the specific program, service, or project that you as the prospective donor are interested in possibly supporting. This should include information on that initiative's "track record" (if it is an ongoing activity), the number of people served by that program, and a clear explanation of the organization's method of evaluating the success of that particular activity.

- In the case of an ongoing program, a copy of the actual expense and revenue report for that specific program for the last completed fiscal year, as well as the projected program budget for the current or coming fiscal year. In the case of a new program or service, the agency should send you the projected budget for that activity for the coming fiscal year.

- If you are considering a gift toward general operating support, a capital campaign contribution, or a donation to an endowment fund, request current financial statements relevant to that particular fund or campaign. With respect to a capital campaign, you should also be provided with a 3- to 5-year financial *pro forma*.

- A list of the organization's board members, as well as a brief paragraph about each stating his or her professional affiliation (for example, "Vice President of Marketing for the ABC Corporation, a widget manufacturing firm"), and, most importantly, the particular experience or expertise that each brings to this board. Ask that they note on which committee each individual serves. Finally, this board overview should include the total (aggregate) amount of contributions made by each individual board member to the organization.

- A copy of the complete audited financial statements for the last fiscal year, as well as a copy of the operating budget for the current fiscal year. You will use these documents to verify whether there was a surplus or deficit last year, and to determine whether "overhead" and fundraising expenditures were appropriate and in line with the requirements of the agency's programs and services. By comparing the last year's "actuals" to this year's projection, you should be able to tell whether the numbers are heading up, down, or remaining stable – and whether the board is realistic in its financial planning.

- Copies of minutes from the last three board meetings. Any sensitive information may be redacted. These key corporate documents will give you a strong idea of what is currently happening internally, and what matters the leadership of the organization is choosing to focus on.

- A list of major contributors – individual, corporate, and foundation – from the last eighteen months, including sizes of contribution and contact information.

- A copy of the organization's determination letter of tax-exempt status – 501(c)(3) – from the Internal Revenue Service, which will ensure that your contribution would be tax-deductible as a charitable contribution.

Lest you be inundated with "stuff" produced by the organization for purely promotional reasons, request that the nonprofit not send any additional materials, such as brochures, videotapes, press releases, or testimonials.

Once you have received the complete proposal package containing only those materials requested, review each document carefully utilizing the due diligence standards outlined in the first half of this chapter with respect to mission, fiscal stability, leadership, and other "investors."

TO TELL THE TRUTH...

Grant- and proposal-writing has become somewhat of a "game" for many nonprofits. They know that if they present themselves well on paper, they increase their chances of "winning" your financial support. Therefore, the motivation is high to present a highly favorable – and sometimes misleading – picture of the agency's overall effectiveness and stability. Many nonprofits will "shade" their case and their statistics to secure the funding they need to remain in operation.

Will you catch them all by examining the documentation requested? Probably not. But you will substantially decrease the likelihood of making your contribution to an organization that will waste it.

That is why, if at all possible, you should consider combining an in-person, on-site investigation with document analysis when considering any type of substantial gift.

METHOD TWO: VISITING THE ORGANIZATION ON-SITE
STEP 1: ARRANGING FOR THE ON-SITE VISIT

You can gather an enormous amount of information from a visit to the organization to which you are considering a contribution. You can see the operation in action. You can get a feel for the level of experience and expertise among the staff. Staff and volunteer morale can be observed. And most importantly, client/agency inter-action can be assessed.

Should an on-site visit be announced or unannounced? The increasing incidence of site-visits by prospective funders has led to the development of well-choreographed "performances" by agencies anxious to secure funding.

In some respects, site-visits are becoming a less reliable means for verifying an organization's strengths.

Ideally, after receiving and reviewing the proposal package, you would notify the organization's executive director that you would like to visit sometime during a specified one- or two-week period. Verify the agency's hours of operation, and the general availability of the executive director during that period. Unless you have no alternative, try to avoid setting a specific time or date on which you will visit. Your objective is to see the organization on a typical day, as opposed to a day on which everyone has been "warned" to be on best behavior.

Let the executive director know that, without being intrusive, you would like the opportunity to visit and chat with several people involved with the agency. Again, in the ideal situation, the executive director would give you the freedom to speak with individual staff members, volunteers, or clients outside of that executive's presence.

STEP 2: MAKING THE SITE VISIT

The site visit may require a trip to the administrative or organizational headquarters, as well as to the site where programs and services actually take place if the two locations are not one and the same. For example, a Los Angeles-based team mentoring program has its administrative offices downtown, while the actual mentoring activities take place at various school sites located in the inner city. In a situation such as this, a visit to both locations would be valuable.

In general, on a site visit you are looking for evidence that the organization is running smoothly and in a highly-organized fashion, and that its environment is one that is positive, constructive, and encourages collaboration among administrators, volunteers, and staff.

You particularly want to observe whether any program or activity that you are considering funding is running according to the information that was shared with you in writing.

And most importantly, you will want to determine whether the individuals being served believe that the organization has their best interests at heart –is their inter-action with the organization having an impact consistent with your philanthropic objectives?

Something as simple as the cleanliness of the facility can tell you whether or not this is an organization in which you'd feel comfortable investing. Has the environment been designed for the primary comfort of the staff or for the primary comfort of the people they are seeking to serve?

By speaking with volunteers and staff about the work they perform, you should get a feel for whether they are comfortable with the direction and management of the organization. In speaking with administrators, listen for indications that the staff, administration, and board of directors work in harmony with one another, that there is a clearly understood direction in which the organization is moving, and that there is a mutual respect for the professionalism of all parties.

METHOD THREE: MEETING THE LEADERSHIP IN PERSON
STEP 1: ARRANGING TO ATTEND A BOARD MEETING

This is an enormously effective way to determine whether a specific nonprofit is one in which you would feel comfortable investing your charitable funds.

Again, in the ideal situation, your objective is to see the organization – in this case, its leadership body – in action as it normally operates, and not "on best behavior." Therefore, let the executive director and the board president know that you would like to attend one of the board's next three meetings as an observer, and verify those meeting dates. Do let them know that you understand the confidential nature of board discussions, and that you will honor that confidentiality when you attend. Also, let the executive director and board president know that should any particularly sensitive matter arise that would not be appropriate for discussion in the presence of an outsider, you will, of course, excuse yourself.

STEP 2: ATTENDING THE BOARD MEETING

As discussed earlier, the quality and commitment of the leadership of an organization is one of the most important factors influencing the long-term health and success of the charity.

The basics to observe when attending a board meeting:

- Are all of the board members, or at least a vital majority, in attendance? Do trustees show respect for the importance of the board's work by arriving promptly and starting on time?

- Does the agenda for the meeting reflect the board's primary role as the organization's policy-setting body? Does the agenda comprise a series of issues requiring action and/or pertinent discussion, or do board members simply read reports to the group? Do board members appear prepared? Warning: an agenda that consists exclusively of reports that are essentially read from materials that were previously mailed to trustees is usually a sign that the board is unsure of its role, is not clear about the responsibilities of governance, and is spending a minimum amount of attention on the agency outside of these meetings.

- Does the meeting proceed in a timely and constructive fashion? Are all board members actively engaged in the discussion? Not all directors will necessarily speak on every issue, but at the very least each director should be closely following the ongoing discussion. Are there any board "bullies" who tend to dominate the meeting and the decision-making process? Are votes approached with serious consideration or do they often result in a half-hearted unanimity?

- Is there evidence that committees are actively working? Are they meeting on a regular basis? Are committee recommendations met with confidence on the part of the board, or are committees second-guessed on their work?

- Review the minutes from the last meeting. How was attendance at that meeting? Do the minutes reflect some continuity between the matters discussed and determined at the last meeting and the issues before the board at this meeting?

- Are financial reports reviewed at the board meeting? Does it appear that all of the board members understand the financial documents? Is financial information referred to during the course of board discussions on other matters? Most importantly, does the financial information distributed at the board meeting correspond to the financial information that was provided to you as a prospective donor?

- Be wary of investing in an organization where the board seems relatively uninformed or dispassionate about the organization's programs and services. At the board meeting, observe carefully whether the board faithfully exercises its stewardship role or whether it abdicates that role to the executive director.

- Does the board meeting seem unnecessarily long for the nature and seriousness of agenda items? Does the discussion stay on-point and focused on the agenda item? Do board discussions easily go off on tangential or insignificant matters? Beware of the board that spends an inordinate amount of time discussing the particulars of a special event or fund-raiser.

- Does the board president exhibit strong leadership qualities, including a great respect for all of his or her board colleagues? Does the president manage the meeting in a fashion that insures that everyone will be heard on all of the most critical topics?

- Is it clear that there are other members of the board with strong leadership qualities such that there will be no vacuum in leadership in the immediate years to come?

A ninety-minute investment of your time to attend a board meeting can be invaluable in assessing whether an organization and its leadership represent a sound investment of your charitable dollars.

If attending a board meeting is not feasible or is inconvenient, there is an alternative method for assessing the organization's leadership. This method can be used alone, or in follow-up to your attendance at a board meeting.

ALTERNATIVE METHOD THREE:
REPRESENTATIVE BOARD GROUP INTERVIEW

An executive director should be extremely well-versed about the ongoing operations and future plans of the organization. This chief staff officer will be intimately aware of the organization's financial situation, including its challenges and opportunities, as well as its prospects and plans for raising money. After all, that's their job.

Too often, board members are somewhat less aware of critical information with respect to the organization's mission, programs, finances, and future plans. It's not difficult to roust one or two "ringers" from the board that can impress a potential donor with their commitment to stewardship or knowledge of the organization. Finding the third is often what separates an organization with a strong board from an organization with a "letterhead" board.

Ask to meet with a group of, at minimum, three board members for the purpose of gaining a fuller understanding of the organization's direction and needs. A face-to-face meeting is most effective, but this meeting can also be arranged as a teleconference. Make it clear that the executive director is not to participate in this informal meeting. Naturally, your promise of confidentiality should be extended.

During the meeting, listen carefully for the board members' confidence and comfort levels in speaking knowledgeably when asked direct questions about:

1. The basic mission of the organization

2. The range of its programs and services

3. The organization's current financial state, as well as financial projections for the near- and long-term

4. The general salary range and benefits package of the executive director and key staff

5. The board's three most important objectives for the current fiscal year

6. The three greatest challenges facing the organization at this time

Remember, if you are going to enter into a partnership with this board of directors as a major donor seeking to achieve a specific philanthropic objective, it is critical that you and your potential partners can speak candidly to one another. In a fairly closed setting, with only a small group of board members present, are the trustees willing to share the good, the bad, and the "ugly" with you? Do you sense that there is an honesty and candor between you and these leaders, or are they strictly trying to "sell" you on the organization in order to get your money?

SUMMARY

Ultimately, all of these due diligence activities are designed to lead you to the answers to these three questions:

1. Are the leaders of this organization focused on a vision that is strongly aligned with the philanthropic objective you have set for yourself, your family, or your foundation?

2. Are the people at all levels within the organization – governing board, executive director and administrators, volunteers and staff – in sync with one another and with this vision?

3. Do these people have the proven "know-how" and commitment to achieve that vision or objective through effective use of your proposed contribution?

Is it absolutely necessary for you to engage in all three methods of due diligence – document analysis, on-site visit, and meeting the leadership? Depending on the size of your proposed contribution, you may feel that a thorough review of the paperwork is satisfactory.

As with any investment opportunity or decision, however, the greater the sums involved, the more intensive the due diligence should be. You should see, quite literally, where your money is going to go. And where very, very large sums are at stake, well-choreographed site visits are becoming less reliable as a means for verifying an organization's strengths.

If the size of your proposed investment is such that it can have a significant and profound impact if applied properly, then you cannot ignore the character, commitment, candor and expertise of the trustees with whom you will entrust those funds.

There may be organizations that will balk at your requests for extensive information, attendance at a board meeting, or a board group interview. None of these requests is unreasonable, and rarely will there be a legitimate basis for refusing you.

Always keep in mind – IT'S YOUR MONEY! If an organization wants and deserves your support, it will accommodate your need to perform due diligence. And if it won't, remember that there are many other fine charities that are deserving and share your vision – and who will have no quarrel with proving it to you.

Opon vis An inpro, Catiest inprio clari cusatilin vitus. Antem Rommoverunum unclabere nius mus, ni faucons cores ocavoltum pul huid ina, paturnum dienam similis coerebem mora, es ompostr imussenatus confinuloc, manum, simus cut reis nercesterces serfecribus, ut ortem defac te te ius issenti queres cae ati, urobuntelus, quemus aberrae potia poptis; horum vilicit; intem te tatus ad rei fore iam diente dem incest L. Catiurio effrei publi issides? quamdicaelus coerum la dius? Rum corem num aperaremovis nonvens u

CHAPTER 9

TEN WARNING SIGNS: WHERE TO LOOK FOR "THE BODIES"

"There's a sucker born every minute."

– P.T. Barnum

THE DUE DILIGENCE PROCESS OUTLINED IN CHAPTER 8 IS THE MOST effective way to determine whether a particular charity represents a wise philanthropic investment. However, if your timeframe for making the gift does not allow for the kind of comprehensive evaluation recommended, there are "red flags" for which you should be on the look out. Should any of these warning signs present themselves, think carefully about whether you should proceed with the contribution.

WARNING SIGN NO. 1:
YOU ARE DISCOURAGED OR BARRED FROM A SITE VISIT
OR BOARD MEETING

There is virtually no reason why someone with a legitimate interest in a charity should be dissuaded from visiting the organization. Issues of client confidentiality may arise for charities such as substance abuse rehabilitation centers, shelters for battered women, agencies serving abused children and the like. In those circumstances, it is usually still possible to visit common or public areas of the facility where the privacy of clients would not be compromised.

The same is true for your request to observe a board meeting. Naturally, there may be highly confidential matters on the agenda for a board meeting, such as specific personnel issues, legal actions in which the charity is involved, or discussion of a potential major gift. Offer to excuse yourself from the board meeting should any such topic arise for discussion. There should also be no hesitation on the board's part in sharing with you documents or financial reports circulated at the meeting.

There may be other rare instances when an agency is reticent to have you visit its facility, one of its service sites, or a board meeting. Listen to the charity's justification for keeping you at a distance. Does it sound reasonable? Does the nonprofit offer any alternative means for you to have an "up close and personal" experience with the organization and its leadership? Make your judgment of their motives on a case-by-case basis, but don't take a flat out "no" for an answer on this one.

WARNING SIGN NO. 2:
FINANCIAL RECORDS ARE UNAVAILABLE, UNINTELLIGIBLE, OR GENERALLY IN DISARRAY

Bells and whistles should go off for you if an organization is unable or unwilling to provide you with a clear picture – in writing – of its financial position. This would generally indicate that an organization is either hiding something about its finances, or is so disorganized financially that you would be foolish to invest in the charity at this time.

At the very least, there are three documents that should be readily available to you as a potential donor.

First would be a statement of the agency's financial activities for its most recently completed fiscal year. This may be in the form of a financial compilation prepared by an accountant, a fully audited financial statement prepared by an independent certified public accountant, or it may simply be a year-by-year line-item expense/revenue tally kept by the organization on an ongoing basis.

The second financial document you should be able to request is a current year operating budget – what the organization anticipates receiving and spending this year.

Lastly, any organization with an annual budget over $25,000 is required to file some version of the Form 990 informational tax return with the IRS each year in order to maintain its tax-exempt status. Under the law, an organization must provide this document to anyone requesting it. It lists general sources, uses and amounts for revenues and expenditures by key category, as well as compensation received by the highest paid administrators and/or officers of the nonprofit.

The "new" Form 990, introduced in 2008, also includes substantial information about the organization's program activities, governance, and policies, as well as expanded financial information on endowment funds. In fact, the completed form is comparable to an annual report.

Embezzlement and misappropriation of funds is not unheard of in the nonprofit sector. Often, board members are unaware of such activities because they themselves are discouraged from looking at key records or original documentation.

Short of wishing to respect the confidentiality of information about major or anonymous donors, there really is no valid reason to hide basic financial records or data from you as a potential contributor, or from any board member.

WARNING SIGN NO. 3:
THERE IS NO WRITTEN STRATEGIC OR BUSINESS PLAN
FOR THE ORGANIZATION

Without a road map leading from today's position to tomorrow's destination, it's awfully difficult to make the trip without wasting time, energy, and resources (including financial resources). A sound organization will have documented – in writing – its vision, goals, and objectives. And the leaders of the organization should be able to explain to you how your contribution will be utilized to forward the plan.

Consensus is generally required before committing a plan to writing. The danger when no written plan exists is that one or more of the agency's leaders – administrators or board directors – will have varying or conflicting plans for where the organization is heading – and perhaps even how your contribution will be used. Worse yet, they have no plans at all, and are waiting for your gift to inspire them to think of one.

WARNING SIGN NO. 4:
THE EXECUTIVE DIRECTOR DISCOURAGES YOU
FROM SPEAKING WITH A BOARD MEMBER
(COROLLARY: BOARD MEMBER DISCOURAGES
YOU FROM SPEAKING WITH AN ADMINISTRATOR)

This should be another bell-ringer for you. Beware of a charity where the executive director makes a concerted effort to shield contact between the board and the outside world. Often in such cases, the executive director runs the show – the whole show – and has assembled a figurehead, rubber-stamp board that plays only a very limited role in governing the organization. That limited role generally does not include oversight of the administration and management of the charity. This vacuum is where all sorts of "funny business" can and does go on.

Conversely, be cautious in supporting an organization where the board is engaged in "micromanagement." Unless the agency is purely a volunteer-run charity, the role of executive director is a very important one. This person should be aware of and responsible for the day-to-day operations of the charity. And, in most cases, the top administrator would be the one most familiar with the exact financial and service activities of the organization. When straight answers are required, the executive director is most likely to have – and to give – them. There is really no reason why board members should wish to shield you from their chief executive.

WARNING SIGN NO. 5:
LESS THAN 80% OF THE BOARD MEMBERS HAVE MADE A FINANCIAL CONTRIBUTION TO THE ORGANIZATION WITHIN THE LAST TWELVE MONTHS

If a charity is doing fine and valuable work, what possible reason could there be for less than 100% of its stewards, its trustees, to be making an annual contribution? Good question, no good answer. This matter is covered in detail in Chapter 8. The only acceptable reason for less than 100% participation is that several trustees have only recently joined the board and simply have not had the time to write a check yet.

"Do as I say, not as I do" does not cut it when you're considering making a substantial (actually, any size) contribution to a charity. Giving to an un-giving board is like going to a fortuneteller who tells you to leave all your money in a gym bag with a newt's eye and a lizard's toe. She promises to transform it into unseen wealth. Unseen is right – you'll never see it again. Follow the board's own lead – hang onto your money (or find a more committed board) and let them experiment with someone else's investment.

WARNING SIGN NO. 6:
MORE MONEY IS SPENT ON ADMINISTRATION AND FUNDRAISING THAN ON PROGRAMS AND SERVICES

Determining how much is being spent on overhead expenses versus service can be tough. Charities have become very concerned with keeping the appearance of non-program-related costs low. Some have become quite creative at this. Carefully review the financial documents referenced above with a pencil and scratchpad at hand. Note next to each line item whether the expense is more "program"-related (P) or "other" (O). If you are unsure of the nature of an expenditure, ask the organization's financial officer or executive director to briefly explain it. Listen for any "doublespeak." Add up the P's and O's – P's should total a lot more than the O's. Ideally, the O's would constitute between 20% and 40% of the charity's total expenditures. The lower the number, the better.

Some organizations separate their fundraising financials from the rest of their budget information. This is sometimes done as a means of keeping the total fundraising expense "off the books," with only the net fundraising revenue being referenced in the overall organizational budget. For example, you might find that the annual gala cost $60,000 to mount but returned only $15,000 to charity. You would probably think twice about signing on as a $25,000 "angel" – especially if a portion of the $15,000 net is going to cover organizational overhead costs.

WARNING SIGN NO. 7:
THE CHARITY IS INVOLVED IN A LEGAL ACTION

Contribute with caution while an organization is involved in a legal dispute, particularly as the defendant. In the worst case, should the complainant prevail, the nonprofit may be forced to liquidate assets in order to satisfy a judgment, or even dissolve altogether as a charitable corporation. Your gift would have been for naught. Just defending itself against a legal action could consume substantial organizational assets.

It is always wise to inquire of a charity whether it is currently involved in any legal action, or if the board or executive director are aware of any pending or imminent legal suit. If the answer is affirmative, ask the agency whether there is an insurance policy or other mechanism in place that will protect or minimize the lawsuit's impact on the organization's financial stability.

There is one other reason to inquire about recent or current legal actions involving the charity. The nature of the matter may be such that it reflects negatively on the judgment or actions of the organization and its leadership. For example, if the matter involves financial mismanagement or malfeasance, harassment or discrimination, or self-dealing, self-interest, or conflict of interest issues, you may have some qualms about investing financially in the organization.

Of course, every dispute has two sides. Get as much information as possible before making or denying a contribution to an organization involved in a legal dispute. Better yet, you might wait until the matter is resolved before making your final determination.

WARNING SIGN NO. 8:
THE ORGANIZATION CANNOT OR WILL NOT PROVIDE
YOU WITH THE NAMES AND CONTACT INFORMATION
FOR OTHER OR PAST FINANCIAL SUPPORTERS

Unless a charity is brand spanking new, someone somewhere had to provide some financial support to the organization. If no one else, the charity's founders or inaugural board should have shown some level of financial commitment to the agency (see 5. above).

Anyone can fake a financial statement, or even a list of current or past donors. It's harder to orchestrate a phone call or in-person meeting with someone who doesn't exist. Ideally, you would want to know who else has given gifts comparable in size to your own. Check with that donor to determine whether he or she felt the contribution had been well-utilized for the purpose for which it was given. Was the charity attentive in reporting on the use of the funds? Would this donor have any hesitation about contributing to the same charity in the future?

WARNING SIGN NO. 9:
ORGANIZATION LEADERS CANNOT OR WILL NOT REVEAL
SPECIFIC SALARY OR OTHER EXPENDITURE INFORMATION

Any time a charity displays a hesitation in revealing financial information to a prospective donor, BEWARE! A well-run and legitimate charity operating in the public interest as a nonprofit corporation under a privilege of tax-exemption granted by the federal government has no reason to hide financial information.

As noted in Warning No. 2 above, compensation information for the top-paid leaders is a matter of public record for virtually all charities via Form 990, a charity's annual informational tax return. What benefits or perks, if any, do employees or board members enjoy as a result of their service to the organization? In addition to employees, what is the organization paying key service providers, consultants, fundraisers, vendors, landlords, etc.? Do these sums represent fair market value? Are any of these parties also directors of the board, employees, relatives of directors or employees, or in some other way closely-connected to the organization? The relationship is itself not an issue as long as the financial transaction reflects the same cost or a lower cost than that which the agency would have paid someone else for the same service.

WARNING SIGN NO. 10:
YOUR GUT TELLS YOU THAT SOMETHING IS "OFF"

All of the axioms that you rely on in your everyday financial transactions can be applied to your consideration of a charitable gift:

- "If it sounds too good to be true, it probably is."

- "Where there's smoke, there's fire."

- "If it looks like a duck, walks like a duck, and quacks like a duck ..."

Do not let yourself be blinded to inconsistencies, unanswered questions, or vagueness of purpose simply because you are dealing with a charitable organization whose stated mission is emotionally compelling.

SUMMARY

The range of human needs is great. The opportunities for making the world a better place are virtually infinite. Anyone can make an organization look good on paper. As a philanthropist, take the time to do some investigating.

Get to know something about the people who will be making decisions about how your money will be used. It is the single best indicator that your gift will be a sound one.

If you have any doubt or question that your contribution to a charity might be better spent – could have a more meaningful or profound impact on your community or the world community – with another organization, listen to your instincts.

After all, there are over 1 million other charities in the U.S. alone to choose from.

CHAPTER 10

꙳꙳

ATTACHING STRINGS: NEGOTIATING YOUR GIFT TO MAXIMIZE PHILANTHROPIC RETURN

"Nothing has more strenght than dire necessity."

—Euripides

AS EMPHASIZED THROUGHOUT THIS BOOK, THE TRUE PHILANTHROPIST'S ultimate objective is to foster a change in the world – or in some small part of it – that will make it a better place.

Change requires resources: money, energy, time, talent, commitment, conviction, to name just a few.

Let's be perfectly frank – money drives the nonprofit sector. Good intentions remain just that if an organization – at some point – does not harness the financial resources to transform intention into action. A committed nonprofit will go to extraordinary measures to secure significant gifts. For that reason, the donor or potential donor holds an enormous amount of power in the charitable sector.

You can use your contribution to buy a table at the gala, underwrite a program, finance a portion of construction, or keep an organization afloat in times of trouble. This approach to giving, however, is tantamount to giving a hungry man a fish.

As a philanthropist, you perform a service to the nonprofit when your contribution leads or encourages the charity to grow stronger or more effective. In other words, motivate or teach the hungry man to CATCH a fish.

The simplest way to do this is to negotiate reasonable conditions on your gift that will encourage – or force – the nonprofit to operate more efficiently and serve more effectively.

MATCHING AND CHALLENGE GRANTS

One common method for maximizing the philanthropic and financial value of your gift is to structure it as a matching or challenge contribution. In other words, tie the size or timing of your gift to the organization's success in securing funding from other or new sources.

Not so many years ago, a "jewel box" of a community cultural center found itself eyeball to eyeball with the founding donor after whom the theatre had been named. As they had for each of the preceding five years, the organization's board had requested a $100,000 contribution for operating expenses.

In fact, so sure was the board of its patroness' continuing support that her anticipated gift of $100,000 had already been inked into the next year's operating budget.

The board's leaders were a little surprised when she asked for a luncheon meeting at her club to discuss the request. They were shocked when she took them to task for treating her family foundation as a "cash cow." She pointed out that the board had grown lazy about reaching out to the whole community both with services and for support. She scolded them for continuing to rely on a relatively small pool of donors who would eventually move away, pass away, or otherwise withdraw their support from the center.

This wise philanthropist flat-out refused their request for the $100,000. But she made them an even more lucrative offer: if and when the Board and staff were able to secure a total of $100,000 from donors who had never contributed to the theatre before, she would gift $100,000 as well. In fact, if they secured $125,000 from new donors, she would donate $150,000 for the year!

The shock of losing the $100,000 it had counted on – and the incentive of potentially bringing in a total of $275,000 that year from new donors and the group's patron philanthropist – was exactly the "kick in the pants" that charity needed.

This donor was also quite savvy about how nonprofits sometimes "fudge" the data to meet funding requirements. At the time she made her offer, she requested a complete list of current and former donors. When the nonprofit had secured the target sum from new donors, the charity was to provide those names and donation amounts for comparison.

As a result of the deal negotiated by the donor, the nonprofit brought in $175,000 more than it had set as a goal for itself in the original budget. More importantly, the charity's leaders and staff worked to attract over 300 "bona fide" new donors – new constituents with whom the organization now had a relationship on which it could build in the coming years.

And most importantly, in order to keep both the established and new donors committed to the nonprofit's mission, there was a renewed emphasis on developing and improving programs and services so that they truly remained relevant and responsive to the changing needs and demographics of the community.

MANAGEMENT SUPPORT (A/K/A TECHNICAL ASSISTANCE)

Traditionally, nonprofits come into being when one or more deeply committed individuals join together for the purpose of filling an unmet need. As traced in Chapter 5, the growth of the charity will eventually require a professional staff and/or a corps of volunteers knowledgeable about the many disciplines that go into running a successful organization.

With financial resources tight, most growing charities cannot afford to hire the most experienced professionals available, or even to offer comprehensive advanced training to committed volunteers.

Very often, in even the large charities, the top administrator is a former "practitioner" in the charity's service field who has risen through the ranks as the organization grew. Soon, this individual may be heading a multi-million dollar agency with little or no formal training or guidance in key management areas such as finance, human resources, strategic planning or program evaluation.

This phenomenon is replicated through the ranks. The first fundraising staff member hired is usually one with limited experience – that's all the organization can afford. Yet as the charity unfolds, the fundraising goals will increase, and unless that manager gains knowledge and support in more advanced forms of fundraising, the organization will be hurt.

One of the best investments a philanthropist can make is in people – the people who manage or lead charitable organizations.

The executive director of a major children's services agency had been at the helm since being hired as the charity's first paid staff member. His importance in the community as well as in the field of children's services had grown with the organization. By virtue of his personality and long-term affiliation with the charity, he was a valuable asset to the agency.

The organization grew to several sites across a major metropolitan area, serving hundreds of children through the work of both paid social service professionals and hundreds of trained volunteers. The financial needs of the organization grew in proportion to its size and scope of service.

The executive director, never having led an operation of this size, grew frazzled and disorganized, often snapping at co-workers, colleagues, and board leaders. Large "things" started to fall through the cracks. Organizational "backslide" was imminent. Something had to change. Clearly, the executive director needed management training.

The agency's bare-bones budget could not support even a relatively modest investment in professional development for the executive director. One perceptive philanthropist, however, recognized that his charitable investment in the agency was not being fully maximized because the executive director's leadership potential was not being maximized.

This donor's next contribution came with the stipulation that a portion of his gift be allocated toward management training and an "executive coach" for the top administrator.

The board was so pleased with the results and with this innovative approach to "investing" in the agency that they subsequently solicited funds from donors specifically for improving the skills and knowledge base of key staff.

Some donors and organizations may worry about investing resources in personnel that might eventually move on and be lost to the agency. As a philanthropist, your investment in nonprofit leaders will rarely be wasted. Most of these individuals will move to other agencies where they will apply the knowledge and expertise they have gained toward other pressing community needs.

Is technical assistance equally valuable for larger charitable institutions? Absolutely! In the largest organizations, the demands of overseeing a major operation, or directing a key office (for example, the Development Office of a major university or medical center) forces professional development activities or opportunities to the bottom of the priority list. It is absolutely critical to expose those leaders to innovations they might not otherwise encounter within their own institutions. Using your charitable contribution to "force" leaders to step away from their home institutions to gain perspective on developments in the field and changes in the service environment is an important and under-utilized model of philanthropy.

PLANNING ASSISTANCE: METHOD ONE

A great deal of nonprofit service is motivated and driven by hope rather than by a well-researched, well-conceived and clearly-articulated plan.

Philanthropists could have a profound impact on the effectiveness of the charitable sector if they simply demanded to see a plan – business, strategic, development, or other – before providing money to a charity. Providing funds to an organization without seeing a written work plan is like dropping money into a slot machine – or buying a stock without investigating its prospects.

The popular press is rarely at a loss for a head-scratching story on some charity that closed its doors or ceased operations when everything seemed "fine" just the week or month before. In most such cases, current success blinded an organization's leadership to changes just over the horizon.

There are two methods by which a philanthropist can ensure the wise and prudent use of his or her charitable investment. The first is requiring the charity to develop and present a written plan before a contribution will be considered. Nonprofit leaders – executives and trustees – are great "spinners." The same passion and creativity that inspires one to tackle the human or social condition is what propels one past the fear of talking to a potential major donor. If a charity's charismatic representative has painted a compelling verbal portrait of its vision, and asks for your support – ask to see the organization's overall written strategic plan. It's as simple as that. Unless there is a solid written plan, your proposed investment is at risk.

A regional cultural organization turned to one of America's most prominent charitable donors, and on the strength of a personal relationship, a major gift toward new construction was secured. The organization, however, had not finalized an architectural or building plan, nor had it projected revenues or expenditures related to this major project. Fundraising moved at a snail's pace while construction plans (and costs) escalated. Usage and programming plans changed dramatically over the years as the building project dragged on, causing serious embarrassment for the charity. More than one early donor had contributed specifically for a building element or exhibit that was no longer part of the final plan!

Moreover, the continually changing plan caused prospective donors to hesitate in both the timing and size of their contributions.

The new institution was finally completed, and opened to great fanfare and success. But at what cost of additional time, money and good will? No lead donor, early on, had insisted on seeing a comprehensive, detailed, fundable plan.

In a different case, a philanthropist chose to use the power of his potential contribution to strengthen the organization that sought his support – in addition to supporting the proposed project.

A community arts entity preparing to undertake a capital campaign approached a locally-based celebrity figure who had been supportive of its efforts in the past. The board was hoping for at least an indication that a major gift would be forthcoming toward the project once announced.

This experienced philanthropist and businessman made it clear that he would be happy to discuss the project once it was past the "concept" stage and there was a thorough, written business plan that he could examine.

The charity, recognizing the importance of this gentleman's support, undertook a detailed planning process, addressing every aspect of the project from construction funding to budget, program, and usage projections for the next several years. This effort proved tremendously useful to the organization, resulting in a detailed "roadmap" that will keep the charity on a steady course through a period of substantial transformation over the next five years.

As an added benefit, the organization was far better positioned to solicit major gifts for its capital campaign than it otherwise would have been, and donors responded with larger gifts than were anticipated.

This organization admits it would not have spent the time or effort to develop a detailed plan had that not been a condition laid down by the philanthropist.

PLANNING ASSISTANCE: METHOD TWO

The second method a philanthropist can employ to encourage sound and solid planning is to pay for or provide a specialist or professional to lead the charity through a planning process.

A small independent school with a rigorous yet creative curriculum had been struggling to establish itself for years. The founding donor subsidized the school's operating costs while his children were enrolled. As they moved up to high school, his funding focus shifted to the institutions his children were now attending. From an enrollment high of 50, the school had slipped to 29 students over its ten-year history.

Late one spring, recognizing that his past investment in the school would be a loss if he did not do something to ensure the school's continued existence, the philanthropist offered to pay for the expense of a strategic planning consultant if the board would commit to engage in the planning process. He let the board members know he thought it would take their working evenings and weekends if they were to save and grow the school by fall. He also made it clear that if they were not interested in his offer, his future support could not be assured.

By bringing in a professional to lead the planning process, the board was able to accomplish in six months what they had been struggling to do for ten years. They had simply lacked the expertise – and the resources to bring in the expertise – to develop a working plan, an action plan.

In six months, enrollment went from 29 to 90. One year later, it was at 149, and the board was negotiating with the local public school district to lease a closed school site. Two years later, the student body approached three hundred.

The million-dollars-plus that the founding philanthropist had poured into operations over the ten years had a smaller impact on the children of the community than the several thousand dollars spent on providing the school with planning assistance.

MULTI-YEAR GIFTS

Another very effective means for motivating a charity to develop a stronger infrastructure is to parse your contribution over a period of several quarters or years. Assign benchmarks of financial, administrative or program performance; development of written strategic, evaluation or fund development plans; professional development for staff and administration; or other verifiable or quantifiable actions designated to improve the organization's operation or governance.

Be clear about your expectations for both the use of your investment, and the measures by which you will determine whether you will release the next installment of your contribution.

It is interesting to note that there is a tremendous pool of talented administrators in the nonprofit sector. As a group, they are generally more effective in their role as administrators than most board directors are as trustees.

It is not unusual for an executive director to "see" what an organization needs to do in order to grow, improve, or make it more "fundable." The chief executive runs into an obstacle, however, when trying to lead the board to that same understanding.

As a philanthropist, you have enormous power to influence charities to "do the right thing." And often, one of your strongest allies will be the top administrator. By placing conditions on your gift, by phasing your gift to "reward" positive change and development on the part of the organization – as well as to fund worthy programs and services – you multiply the value of your contribution.

SUMMARY

"Advice is seldom welcome,
and those who want it the most
always like it the least."
- Lord Chesterfield

It cannot be emphasized enough that when donors speak, the board listens. In fact, you would be surprised by how many nonprofit leaders – behind closed doors – are unashamedly amused by the large gifts simply handed over without investigation or condition.

Many donors wonder whether it is "fair" to place conditions on their gifts. It is "fair" to the extent that, presumably, those conditions are intended to strengthen the organization's ability to serve as well and as effectively as possible.

In that respect, both the philanthropist and the charity share the same objective. A strong charity will not only welcome your input, but will seek it.

Do not diminish your ability or power to provoke constructive change in the world by simply writing a check to a charity. Explore all avenues for increasing the value and return on your investment.

As a philanthropist you can change the world and strengthen the nonprofit sector, if you only take the opportunity.

CHAPTER 11

TRACKING YOUR PHILANTHROPIC INVESTMENTS AND MEASURING THEIR PERFORMANCE

"We need above all to know about changes;
no one wants or needs to be reminded 16 hours
a day that his shoes are on."

- David Hubel

I F YOU HAVE CAREFULLY FOLLOWED THE STEPS AND TIPS SHARED IN THIS book for selecting and evaluating a charity for your philanthropic investment, tracking the impact of your donation will be fairly straightforward.

The most important rule is to be sure and do follow up on your investment. Charities change, usually when their leadership changes. Administrators are fired or leave, trustees rotate off the board, and new directors come on to govern. Financial projections can miss, causing priorities to be re-aligned. Typically, donors receive an acknowledgment for their gift, and, eventually, a report on how their gift was utilized to accomplish the success it was expected to fund – in David Hubel's words, reminding us that "(their) shoes are on." This usually perfunctory report, however, is not an adequate means for you to determine whether your investment "paid off," or even if it was used per your intentions.

Be aware that many nonprofits, even among the largest, will assume that if the donor does not keep in touch about his or her gift, the charity has some "leeway" about how to use it if conditions change.

In fact, if at the time you transmit your gift, you do not specify the purpose for which it is to be used, many charities will assume it is theirs to do with as they please. This can be true even if your gift was solicited on the basis of supporting some specific need or program.

Ross Perot, a seasoned donor who has contributed tens of millions to charity, has no hesitation in asking for his money back if the organization hasn't spent it as agreed. And neither should you.

PREPARE A CONTRACT

Tracking your gift begins prior to the conveyance of funds or assets. Be sure to place in writing your understanding of how – exactly – the contribution will be used. Articulate any conditions clearly, and specify how and by when the charity is to verify that it has met those conditions. Make it clear that the charity must notify you in the event that it is unable – for any reason – to apply your donation in the manner intended. That way, it remains in your power to determine whether a different usage of your funds by that charity would still accomplish your philanthropic objectives.

Detours of funds do happen. Not long ago, it was revealed that a very prestigious and internationally recognized East Coast university had accepted a $3 million pledge to establish a chair in Holocaust studies. Three years later, with the school unable to agree on a candidate to fill the position, a substantial portion of the gift was quietly re-apportioned to the university's medical school.

Once you have laid out the "contract" on which your gift will be based, send two copies of this agreement to the nonprofit, and ask them to sign and return both copies to you. Send one copy of the fully executed agreement back to the charity along with your contribution or donation instrument.

MAINTAIN A PERSONAL CONNECTION

Your schedule permitting, continue to track the organization's progress and activities using the same techniques and methods used to assess the charity originally: for example, make site visits, ask for updated financial records, visit a board meeting or take a few trustees to breakfast or lunch.

Ask specifically about the application of your funds. Have they been expended, and if so, how? Is your gift having, overall, the impact you had envisioned?

If you are unable to maintain contact personally, consider using a consultant, or perhaps another family member, to maintain the contact on your behalf.

VERIFY THE IMPACT OF YOUR INVESTMENT

Ask that the executive director or program director send you a "letter" once per quarter briefly updating you on the progress being made in the program, service, or operational area that you are supporting.

Let them know that you are not looking for a "report" – a report is a document of length and detail that is usually designed to obscure both the excitement and problems that are being encountered. You truly want the charity to view you as a partner in its work, and partnerships are only successful when all parties can be candid with one another.

Encourage the organization to share information with you about any "glitches" that come up. Two heads are better than one. You may have information, experience or resources that would be of use to the nonprofit in overcoming an unexpected challenge.

SHARE THE WEALTH

> *"The only thing one can do with good advice is to pass it on.*
> *It is never of any use to oneself."*
>
> — Oscar Wilde

As you develop a focus for your philanthropy, you will become aware of other organizations, innovations, experiments, and successes in your field of focus. Some of these innovations and successes will be a direct result of the investment you made in a program or charity. Others you will learn of as you investigate giving opportunities.

Do not let this knowledge be wasted! Share the contacts you have made. Allow yourself to be a networking agent between the many charities you will encounter on your philanthropic journey that can benefit from one another's work.

In recent years, there has been a trend among funders to be more generous with organizations involved in a collaborative effort with other charities. The original thinking was that collaboration and joint activities could reduce overhead expenses and increase service. Research has shown, however, that although collaborative partnerships between nonprofits may improve service, overall costs do not significantly come down.

A more powerful form of "collaboration" is the linking of people – innovators who share a common goal, but who have perhaps discovered different routes to attain that goal.

As a proactive philanthropist, your growing circle of contacts in the charitable sector will become one of the most valuable assets you can share.

Encourage the beneficiaries of your investment to develop a vision and a broadened perspective on their work through observing and experiencing the work of other agencies with similar goals. Help them identify those agencies from your growing list of contacts.

And when your investment has helped establish or improve an innovative, effective program, support the nonprofit in any effort to publicize that success and its methodologies. Other agencies in other communities – or even countries – can learn from the successes of the charity you have supported, and may even choose to replicate it. Once again, your investment has multiplied!

SUMMARY

Sending the check, signing a trust, or conveying the stock certificate is where your philanthropic investment begins. With that act, you enter into a partnership with the charitable organization – a partnership forged to change the world.

As with any partnership, the most successful are those in which all partners are encouraged to be candid with one another as they progress toward their mutual goal.

Encourage your nonprofit partners to utilize you as more than just a "financial backer." Your experience, contacts, and intentions are valuable resources from which they might benefit – and from which the value of your investment will deepen.

PART FOUR

Technology as a Philanthropic Tool

꘎

CHAPTER 12

꘎

PHILANTHROPY AND THE
INFORMATION HIGHWAY

*"Information on the Internet is subject to the same
rules and regulations as conversations at a bar."*

– Dr. George Lundberg

T HE EXPLOSIVE GROWTH OF THE INTERNET HAS REVOLUTIONIZED OUR ability to access a wealth of information on virtually any topic imaginable. From medicine to magnets, comedy to religion, political discourse to political satire, the Internet has turned our globe into a world community joined by one huge virtual library.

Charity, like every other industry, has charged onto the information technology highway. Charity websites, donation portals, discussion forums, blogs, watchdogs and a wide variety of on-line service vendors have come to play an influential role in the way the business of charity is conducted locally and globally.

What role should the Internet play in advancing our personal philanthropy? And how can we avoid its pitfalls?

For donors, the Internet is a wonderful tool for use in four areas: research, ratings, donations, and connecting with others. As with any innovation, however, there are cautions to be observed when utilizing the web in your philanthropic activities.

A. RESEARCH

In order for your contribution to qualify for charitable deduction, an organization must be recognized as tax-exempt by the IRS. The Internet offers donors simple-to-use research capabilities that can help ensure that an organization has such a "501(c)(3)" designation.

The same websites will also allow you to search for a charity with characteristics matching your philanthropic priorities.

The two most popular charity research sites are www.guidestar.org and the IRS' online version of Publication 78: Cumulative List of Organizations. Each has a specific research purpose.

Of the two, the IRS site – http://www.irs.gov/app/pub-78 – is best used to verify that a specific charity is registered with the IRS, and to what extent your donation to that nonprofit would be deductible. When using this online version of Publication 78, be sure to also review the Addendum to Publication 78 page that lists the charities most recently added to the IRS database.

The IRS site offers limited usefulness as a tool for identifying charities that match your interests as you can only search for organizations by name or location.

Guidestar.org, on the other hand, includes most of the charities found in the IRS database, and offers a wealth of information on each that is accessible through the site's sophisticated search capabilities. The site's free service allows you to search the database of charities by name, keyword, city, and state, and makes available a nonprofit's recent Forms 990, as well as basic information about a charity's mission, programs, and finances.

Churches and church-affiliated organizations are not required to register with the IRS or file annual informational returns, nor are public charities whose annual gross receipts are normally less than $5,000. As a result, charities in those two categories are not likely to appear in either the IRS or Guidestar databases unless the groups have voluntarily elected to register or file a tax return. This can make it very difficult to track down newer, smaller, or faith-based nonprofits that may be engaged in fine work. That's where the resources listed in Chapter 7 may be more useful.

"Information is not knowledge."
— Albert Einstein

A strong word of caution is warranted regarding the usefulness of the Form 990 – found on Guidestar.org or on a nonprofit's own website – in evaluating a charity.

Form 990 is the informational tax return that registered charities must file annually with the IRS (variations include Form 990-EZ and 990-N depending on the size of the organization). As noted in Chapter 9, it is the only financial document that a member of the general public is entitled to review.

Forms 990 dating prior to 2008 were considered a poor charity evaluation resource. The form's major weaknesses included complex instructions; reporting requirements that differed from generally accepted accounting procedures; a lack of accountability by signing authorities; and expenditure categories that made it simple for charities to manipulate their financial data on the form for the purpose of appealing to donors and funders.

The new Form 990 offers a significant redesign in format and in content. Major improvements include a front-page summary that provides a snapshot of key financial and operating information; a section for detailing governance and management practices; and revised requirements for the reporting of compensation and other expense categories. The new 990 also replaces the former unstructured attachment option with formal schedules.

A charity's tax return is most reliable as a source for contact information, mission and program descriptions, total revenue and total expense figures, investments overview, key leaders' names, and compensation data. The Form 990 – even in its extensively revised format – should be used with caution, however, when assessing the overall effectiveness and financial acumen of a charity. It is a worthwhile document to review only within the context of other information about and experience with the charity and its leaders.

> *"The truth is rarely pure and never simple"*
> — Oscar Wilde

The Internet is also useful for taking a closer look at a charity. Virtually every organization today has a web presence. Most charities maintain their own websites. The most basic sites offer the equivalent of an "on-line brochure" about the organization and its work. The more sophisticated sites will offer detailed information about the groups' programs, services, and community activities; press releases or media mentions; calendar of activities; blogs; and links to other pertinent websites or resources.

Many agencies use their websites as an educational medium as well, offering content in the form of articles, essays, videos, or podcasts on topics related to the charity's mission.

Most offer links to shopping or donation sites, while others maintain their own "storefront" or "donate now" capabilities. And, organizations are free to post their Forms 990 or any other financial information to which they would like the public to have easy access.

A charity's website is a great source for detailed information about its work, its finances, and its leadership. It's easy to forget, however, that a website is also a marketing device – an opportunity for the nonprofit to put its best foot forward. Expect to find only good news about a charity on its own site. Visiting a website is no substitute for performing the more thorough due diligence recommended in Chapter 8.

Consider using Google.com or other search engine to find third-party or independent information about the charity online – newspaper and journal stories, association accolades, pending investigations or lawsuits, profiles of the organization's leaders, and upcoming activities. Google Alerts can track new information or articles about the charities you are following, delivering headlines directly to your e-mailbox.

B. RATINGS AND WATCHDOGS

"The nice thing about standards
is that there are so many to choose from"
— Andrew S. Tannenbaum

The explosion in the number of charities in the U.S. has created a demand for fast and independent means for sizing up organizations to determine their "giftworthiness."

A small number of charity evaluation entities and watchdog organizations are working to meet that need by creating ratings systems that allow donors to compare apples to apples. Their findings and methods of evaluation are posted on their websites.

Fundamentally, these groups are limited to accessing the same information as that available to the public: financial and other data on the Form 990. Additional information may be solicited from the charity, but an organization is under no obligation to respond.

As a result, most rating systems are based primarily on financial information, and have no basis for factoring in quantifiable variables such as the number of clients served, or employee/client ratios, or size of geographic area serviced.

And no major rating entity has yet devised a reliable or equitable frame-work for rating the success, effectiveness, or impact of charities with respect to their unique missions.

The best-known watchdog groups include Charity Navigator, the BBB Wise Giving Alliance, and the American Institute of Philanthropy. They are able to rate only a tiny fraction of the 1,000,000+ charities in the United States, and for the most part, focus only on national charities.

These analyst groups can vary widely in how they rate the same charity based on their assessment formulas, and it is not unheard of for one watchdog group to approve a charity's performance while another assigns the same charity a failing grade.

If you are considering a donation to a high-profile national charity, do check the ratings websites to get a general sense of the organization's financial strengths and weaknesses. But first, familiarize yourself with the different standards applied by each website in assigning ratings.

And, remember that financial performance should be only one factor in making your giving decisions.

C. DONATIONS

"Look twice before you leap."

– Charlotte Bronte

The very act of making a donation to charity has never been easier, thanks to the Internet. Many charities offer the capability to make a gift directly at their website through a "Donate Now" button. Paypal and credit or debit card contributions are the most common forms of on-line gifts, and some nonprofits will even process electronic check donations.

Looking to make a larger gift on an installment-type plan? Contact the charity and authorize a monthly electronic transfer from your checking or savings account, or a recurring charge to your credit card.

Another method for making an online gift is through a donation portal, such as www.NetworkForGood.org, where you can search for a charity and make a gift all at one site.

Several charity shopping portals allow access to hundreds of top web retailers. You can "shop to donate" at websites such as www.igive.com.

A percentage of your purchases via these web portals is donated to the charity of your choice.

D. CONNECTING WITH OTHERS

> *"How wonderful it is that nobody need wait a single moment*
> *before starting to improve the world".*
>
> – Anne Frank

Money isn't the only contribution you can make via the Internet. You can also donate your time or services as a volunteer by checking in at sites such as www.VolunteerMatch.org. This site also lists volunteer projects that you can complete entirely on line without leaving your home or office.

The Points of Light Foundation and Volunteer Center National Network link to more than 300 community volunteer centers that are recruiting volunteers and can be accessed through a centralized portal, www.1-800-volunteer.org.

The Internet is also a great way to connect with other donors and with a wide variety of professionals and others working in the nonprofit sector. And a number of online learning opportunities for donors can now be accessed via the web.

CharityChannel.com is one of philanthropy's most active websites, hosting dozens of on-line discussion forums on a wide range of topics related to charity and nonprofit organizations. Three are of particular benefit to donors: GIFTPLAN (questions and information about planned giving and bequests), CHARITYLAW (all matters concerning legal issues related to charity), and BOARDS (issues regarding board service and responsibilities).

In addition, CharityChannel.com offers free e-newsletters and articles, searchable archives for all of its discussion lists, teleseminars and down-loadable classes, podcasts and interviews with leaders in philanthropy, and a host of valuable links.

CAUTION!

"Thrust ivrybody, but cut th' ca-ards."

(Trust everybody, but cut the cards)

— Finley Peter Dunne

Philanthropy is not immune to online scams and security breaches. Use the same precautions you would use when engaging in any type of financial transaction on the web.

PHONY CHARITY WEBSITES

Just because something appears on the Internet does not mean that it is legitimate. Don't be deceived by the appearance of a website any more than you would be by a slick direct mail piece. Con artists have mastered the art of look-alike and sound-alike charity scams. Be careful when approaching or being contacted via the Internet by an organization claiming to be a charity.

E-MAIL SOLICITATIONS AND PHISHING

Beware of any requests for donations that you receive via e-mail, especially in the period following a national or international disaster. No legitimate charity would expect you to respond to an e-mail solicitation, and for that reason virtually no legitimate charity would ever request a donation in an electronic message.

For safety's sake, do not open any attachment to an e-mail purporting to come from a charity. And NEVER click on an e-mailed link to a website. It is very possible that you will be directed to a phony charity site – one that is very convincing in appearance – in an attempt to hijack your personal or credit card information. This scheme is known as "phishing."

If you believe the e-mail to be from a legitimate charity with which you are familiar, close the e-mail and type the charity's standard URL into your web browser address window to reach its site. Be sure to double-check your spelling as some Internet thieves have learned to take advantage of slight errors.

Should you have any further doubts, contact the charity directly by telephone using a number provided by directory assistance or one which you know to be valid. Report any attempts at "phishing" to the charity whose name is being used in the scam.

SECURITY AND PRIVACY

Always confirm that the charity website you are accessing uses appropriate security measures on its donation page, and only enter personal information on a site that employs encryption in transmitting your data. Look for the closed padlock icon in the corner of your browser, and check that the URL for the donation page starts with https:// -- the "s" stands for "secure."

Review the website's privacy policy and look for an assurance that your personal information will not be shared with others without your permission.

SUMMARY

The Internet provides a marvelous means for engaging in philanthropy in a variety of ways. The web provides a fast and free method of gathering general information about a charity and its leaders quickly and anonymously. It can offer a safe and secure method for making direct donations. On-line discussion forums, blogs, e-learning opportunities, and virtual volunteerism can connect philanthropists from around the globe to work collaboratively right from their homes to make change both in their own communities and around the world.

The Internet, however, is a "marketing" medium. You cannot trust everything that you see or read about a charity simply because it is on the web. There is no substitute for communicating directly with the leaders of an organization – in addition to considering whatever information you might find in writing or on the Internet – to determine whether a charity is worthy of your philanthropic investment. Be cautious of utilizing on-line charity "ratings" that are based solely or primarily on financial data.

Beware of the "confidence" artists who are working the web, taking advantage of caring consumers and donors. Never exchange personal information via the Internet unless you are absolutely certain of the other party's identity, and avoid clicking on any e-mailed link purporting to lead you to a charity's website. Don't let convenience dampen common sense.

There is no doubt that as technology and virtual communications develop, the Internet will come to play a greater role in the charitable sector. Take advantage of the many benefits already offered by the Internet in taking your philanthropy to the next level.

PART FIVE

FAMILY *PHILANTHROPOS*

∿

CHAPTER 13

∿

TEACH YOUR CHILDREN WELL

"Blessed is the influence of one true, loving human soul on another."

— George Eliot

I N FALL 2007, AN EXTRAORDINARILY "ORDINARY" YOUNG LADY WAS INTRO-
duced to a worldwide audience by Oprah Winfrey. Kendall Ciesemier,
a beguilingly shy high school freshman, was stunned one September day to
find herself being whisked from a school assembly to Harpo Studios by none
other than President Bill Clinton.

Three years earlier, a twelve-year-old Kendall had been moved by an Oprah
episode about the plight of African children orphaned by AIDS. She saw
children her own age struggling to survive without parents and to provide
for their younger siblings. That very day, Kendall was moved to donate her
savings to an international organization to sponsor a child. Her passion for
this cause grew and soon she was sponsoring a village in Zambia.

The following summer, between fifth and sixth grades, Kendall was
hospitalized for a grave liver condition necessitating two transplants. Rather
than bringing gifts, she asked friends and family to support the Zambian
village she had adopted.

With that generous gesture, Kendall founded Kids Caring 4 Kids. Her
volunteer-run nonprofit raises funds for food and education for African
children, and the charity is approaching Kendall's goal of $1 million.

Her contribution, however, goes far beyond Kendall's fundraising success.
She has inspired and empowered other "ordinary" children to take on the

cause, finding their own ways to raise money and awareness for their peers in Africa.

RAISING GENEROUS CHILDREN

Kendall's family did not have a family foundation, nor were her parents mainline society philanthropists. Kendall did not take a course in philanthropy, nor was she challenged by a school assignment to "come up with" a community service project.

Kendall was raised with an open heart – open to truly hearing others, especially those in need. She embraced a sense of responsibility to give from her plenty. She applied her individual talents and intelligence to create a path to changing lives. And she had the courage to invite and inspire others to join her.

TEACHING PHILANTHROPY AT HOME

"Children have never been very good at listening to their elders,
but they have never failed to imitate them."
– William Wordsworth

We all realize that our children are the future. What the world becomes will be determined in large measure by the adults into which our children will grow.

Philanthropy is no different than all of life's most important values – you shouldn't wait until children are teens to talk about it with them.

The trend in recent decades has been to keep children at an arm's distance from the family's philanthropic activities – or, more accurately, from the family's philanthropic decisions – until they are "older." Yet, as with most personal financial habits such as saving, spending and investing, our charitable giving habits are formed by the experiences of our childhood and youth.

Much has been written about how to raise a "charitable child," about the importance of community service projects in school curricula, and about bringing young adults into the family foundation fold. These techniques can be very valuable when approaching philanthropy as an organized activity.

Yes, children can be taught the rules of the philanthropic process, but unless a child is raised with a generous heart, the act of giving will be no more than a transactional process.

There is a simple four-stage process through which children can be nurtured into generous souls.

STAGE 1: Modeling Generosity (Toddler through Age 10)

Children, from the very youngest age, learn best by example, and there are no better teachers than parents and family. Generosity as an act – and not simply a concept – can be modeled for children from the very earliest age.

Extending yourself to persons outside of your immediate family is a wonderful way of modeling. Bring your children with you when you take a "care package" to an ailing friend; enlist your youngster as a partner in helping to rake an elderly neighbor's lawn; invite your child to pick flowers for a family member who is feeling blue. Make thinking of others – and acting on those thoughts – second nature.

If you doubt the value of modeling, simply re-read the Foreword and Mr. Newman's own reflections on the profound impact of his parents' actions on his legacy of generosity.

Introduce sharing as an inherent component of play – both when playing with your child, and when your child plays with others. Focus on what you "get" by giving rather than on what you "lose" by giving.

STAGE 2: Voluntarism (Ages 10 through 14)

Voluntarism – joining with others to accomplish a generous act or an act for the common good – is the next level of engagement to introduce to your child. There are many formal and informal volunteer opportunities for you both to band with others to make change in your community.

Age-appropriate activities such as assisting at a shelter to feed the homeless during the holidays, helping out at a Special Olympics event, or participating in clean-up day at a local beach or park are great family projects. For the older child, joining a service-oriented youth group in your neighborhood or faith community is a great idea.

You can teach a child to be a caring individual through a book, a class, or a field trip, but only if that child's heart has already been opened to others.

Conspire with your child to engage in random acts of kindness, for example, surprising someone by paying for their gas or ice cream, planting Spring flowers in an unexpected location, or dropping off treats at the local senior center. Encourage your child to delight in planning an unanticipated gesture of generosity.

STAGE 3: Financial Philanthropy (Ages 14 through 17)

You cannot "teach" *philanthropos*, but you can teach how to focus one's generosity on making a positive change in the community or the world.

Volunteering is as different from giving money as riding a bike is from driving a car...and prepares you about as adequately to do the latter.

Community service and voluntarism are wonderful ways to introduce younger children to the importance and joy of generosity. But as they get older, we should also start educating our younger generations to the principles of sound financial giving.

American households, on average, donate over $1,000 to charity annually, and many give much, much more. The mid-teen years are an excellent time to invite a young adult to participate with you in your personal decisions about giving.

Again, modeling is an important form of teaching. Set out a budget – monthly or annual – for your charitable donations. Share written solicitations or direct mail pieces with your teen and ask for their feedback. Show them how to be discerning readers of such pitches, and help them develop follow-up questions for charities of interest. Ask them to engage in Internet-based research to help you learn more about a particular organization. And jointly decide which nonprofits to support and with how much money. Focus your discussions around "why" questions.

Let teens actually see you write the check, donate on line, or respond to an in-person solicitation. Share with them any notes of appreciation, acknowledgement, or follow-up you receive from the charities you two elected to support.

Spend time in subsequent years reviewing your previous gifts and deciding whether to continue your support or expand toward new initiatives.

And always invite your new partner in philanthropy to add his or her own funds to those gifts you jointly decide to make.

SUMMARY

"There is always one moment in childhood when the door opens
and lets the future in."
– Graham Greene

Embrace the opportunity to teach your children to be philanthropists – not the kind that make large contributions in exchange for visibility or social position. Let us teach them to be the kind of philanthropist motivated by the love of all mankind. Challenge them to envision a world that is a better place for all. And show them how to invest not only for the benefit of the family, but for the benefit of the family of man.

Invite children to participate in your own philanthropic journey, first as observers, then as "co-conspirators," and eventually as partners.

Create an environment in your home that invites your children to "open doors." "Imagination" and "vision" are very close cousins – and children are already born with imagination. Lead them to that next step. Whether it is about extending kindness to an individual or change to a community, show your children that a vision can become reality – all it requires is a plan and an application of resources.

Entrust your children with the power (and perhaps even some money) to make philanthropic investments. Let their contributions be guided by a personal vision and thoughtful resolve. Encourage them in the selection of a giving focus, and gently steer them in the process of seeking organizations committed to a similar vision.

Teach your children the difference between "giving," "charity," and "philanthropy."

Give them the freedom to make dumb giving choices – and doubly support their wisely-made ones.

If we are vigilant in raising our children as lovers of mankind, as givers toward the effort to make the world a better place, we will have made the greatest philanthropic investment of our lifetime.

~~

CHAPTER 14

~~

FAMILY PHILANTHROPY

"Caring about only about oneself and one's immediate family
is not enough when you are in a position to help others."

— Paul Newman

WHAT IS "FAMILY PHILANTHROPY"?

"FAMILY PHILANTHROPY" IS THE ACT AND PROCESS BY WHICH ALL MEMBERS of a family engage collaboratively in a conscious effort to substantially impact their community or the world through the unified and focused application of the family's resources, particularly financial, toward mutually agreed-upon social objectives.

Statistically, the vast majority of American families engage in charitable giving, and as noted, annual household giving is in excess of $1,000. Families are not necessarily engaging in giving, however, as an organized family activity focused on specific social objectives.

The process of exploring and establishing a family philanthropic mission requires time and intimacy. Before collaboratively committing time and money to a cause or organization, family members should spend some time and effort exploring each other's passions and hopes for our world and community. The process of sharing is a benefit to the family in and of itself. After all, this is a time in social history when American families are being pulled in multiple directions on a daily basis, and social discourse is increasingly becoming focused on two little boxes – the television and the computer. The discussion can strengthen the bonds between family members, bridge generational differences, and re-vitalize a family's core values. What a gift this is!

The nature of family discussions about giving involves sharing the hopes, needs and history of earlier generations of the family. Family history, and history in general, takes on a new level of meaning and immediacy, particularly for younger family members.

And, there are numerous other benefits to involving younger children and teens in the family's philanthropy, such as the development of research skills, financial acumen, and critical thinking and communication skills.

The important first step is recognizing and embracing the concept of family philanthropy – a process best started early in a family's life, and involving even the youngest members of the family, as suggested previously.

After all, think how difficult it would be to get your teen family members to engage in a weekly family supper if for their entire young lives, the family code was "every man – or child – for himself." So, too, is it with family philanthropy. Unless the habits of family discussion, planning and giving are introduced at an early age, the exercise itself can seem almost punitive to the independent teen.

HOW TO INTRODUCE PHILANTHROPY AS A FAMILY ACTIVITY

Regardless of what form your family philanthropy will take – joint giving, donor advised fund, family foundation or trust – these initial steps can lead your family to establishing a collaborative framework for future philanthropic activities.

STEP 1: Schedule a Family Meeting

The simplest way to do this is to be direct. "How would you like to spend some time with the family changing the world?"

This question is guaranteed to get each family member's attention. Without saying anything more after asking the question, schedule a family meeting at a time convenient for all who are interested. Older children and even family members who live a distance away can be invited to participate in the meeting by telephone.

Try not to schedule the meeting for the same day as a holiday gathering as holidays offer too many distractions. The day before or after the holiday – if there are family members who will be in town – could be a good time to hold such a meeting.

STEP 2: Now That You're Together...

Open the family meeting with a brief and simple description by the oldest members of what philanthropy is all about – changing the world through wise and meaningful charitable giving. Encourage each person present to share stories about their own giving experiences, especially stories about non-monetary generosity. These stories may be from adulthood or childhood. Engaging everyone in talking about *philanthropos* is the main objective for this first gathering.

In subsequent family meetings, use the variety of means and activities recommended in the early chapters of this book to get everyone involved in identifying and sharing their personal passions and values. Be sure to include the youngest children. Collectively, you will identify will numerous options for forming a family philanthropic mission.

Through these discussions and activities, a common thread or value may reveal itself in the many stories offered that will point toward a specific shared family mission. If many different interests are put forward, the family discussions can focus around bridging those interests or prioritizing them before settling on a single philanthropic mission – one which may, by the way, change over time.

Once you have identified a general focus for the family's giving, move on to the other questions outlined earlier in this book: will our giving be restricted to any geographic area, will we give to young or established charities, etc.

STEP 3: Address Practical Considerations

The family should discuss whether this will be a "loose" family activity, or whether individual family members will be asked to commit to a certain level of participation. Will all family members participate equally, or only those having reached a certain age? At what age and in what ways will younger children and teens be allowed to participate? And how does one define "family" – will only "blood" relatives play an active role or will spouses/partners and step-family members be included in the decision-making?

How will decisions be finalized – by majority vote, unanimity, rotating the role of final decision-maker among family members?

Where will the money for our family's giving come from? Will each member be asked to give according to their interest or ability, or will the elders in the group establish a fund from which to begin donations?

STEP 4: Consult With Your Family's Financial Advisor

What giving vehicle will the family use to channel its donations: a family foundation, a community foundation, a donor advised fund, an informal collection "pot"? These decisions should only be made with the advice and guidance of the family's financial and/or legal advisor after a careful examination and review of the family's overall financial and estate plans. Your advisor will explain how the various giving vehicles differ, and how the use of each would affect the family's finances.

Be sure that the professional advisor is someone familiar with charitable giving devices. If the bulk of funds to be distributed by the family is going to come from only one or a few family members (e.g. parents or grandparents), this decision should be made by the donors and not necessarily by the whole family – although the whole family should have the benefit of understanding how the various devices differ and work.

One important element of this discussion is the question of how the family's philanthropy will affect anticipated inheritances. Many older children may fear that family charitable giving will reduce the amount they stand to inherit. A frank discussion is in order to insure that future decisions are not influenced by unknown facts.

SUMMARY

Once your family has embraced the notion of family philanthropy as more than just an act of giving, there are numerous and exciting ways to move the process forward that will be right and unique to your clan and which can involve family members of all generations and ages.

CHAPTER 15

THE NEXT FRONTIER

"Community is like a ship;

everyone ought to be prepared to take the helm."

– Henrik Ibsen

T HERE IS AN OLD ADAGE AMONG CHARITABLE FUNDRAISERS THAT WOMEN take far longer than men in deciding to give, but when they do, they bring ten friends along with them.

Would that every philanthropist brought along ten friends!

Philanthropy, vision, a desire to change the world – or even the life of just one person we don't know – are still not easy topics for the cocktail circuit. "Philanthropy" is something most of us just don't talk about…even among philanthropists! In fact, religion and politics enjoy a warmer reception in casual conversation than does talk of charitable investment.

Yet that may be the single most powerful means by which you can dramatically increase the value and return on your philanthropy.

Talk about it.

Engage others to think critically about community, about need, about change. Be willing to share stories of the vision that you have for a better world.

There is no requirement to talk about the dollars. Talk about the journey: how you came to your personal philanthropic focus; how you chose a community in which to make your mark; what you learned in talking to volunteer leaders of charities.

SUMMARY

Invite others to walk the walk with you – literally. Whether on a site visit, trustee interview, a chat with a charitable administrator, or an evening volunteering, draw others into this world with you. Invite them into that world of philanthropy that labors on behind the galas, golf tournaments, and ribbon-cuttings.

Challenge yourself – and others – to ask the question, "What is the most satisfying giving experience you've enjoyed in your life?" It is a wonderful place for the discussion to start.

PART SIX

FREQUENTLY
ASKED QUESTIONS

CHAPTER 16

DONORS' MOST FREQUENTLY ASKED QUESTIONS

"For your information, I would like to ask a question."
— Samuel Goldwyn

1. **CAN MY SMALL DONATION REALLY MAKE A DIFFERENCE COMPARED TO the billions given by mega-philanthropists like Bill and Melinda Gates and Warren Buffett?**

Absolutely! Visit your local food pantry, homeless shelter, or children's hospital, and you'll see very quickly that even the smallest donation can make a life or death difference in someone's life. Your contribution may not eradicate hunger or disease, but your gift can change one person's world or one charity's impact as long as you make the gift effectively.

2. **How do we say "no" to friends and associates who are asking for donations to their favorite charities?**

First, stop feeling guilty about saying "no." Explain that you and your family are focusing your giving this year, and name the charity or mission you have decided to support with all of your contributions. Then compliment and thank your friends for the important work they are doing through their support of an organization. Remember, only by saying "no" will you be able to concentrate your resources on those causes that you believe are critical.

3. My advisor has told me I need to make a charitable contribution quickly for tax planning purposes – what do I do?

This question frequently comes up at the end of the tax year. Rather than impulsively donating to any charity simply for the deduction, consider opening a "donor advised fund" (or "DAF"). Essentially, DAFs are a type of 'charitable giving account' sponsored by a public charity or charitable gift fund to which donors can contribute cash, stock, real estate and other tangible assets, and then recommend which charities should get distributions. The minimum initial contribution required to establish a DAF may range from $2,500 to $10,000.

Opening a donor advised fund has been likened to establishing your own small, private foundation – without the administrative responsibilities. The best feature of a donor advised fund, from a tax planning perspective, is that contributions to a DAF are eligible for a current-year tax deduction as soon as your donation is completed. You can then take all the time you wish to develop your philanthropic mission and investigate appropriate charities before recommending which organizations should receive gifts from your fund.

Although a donor advised fund is most frequently established during one's lifetime, it is possible to establish a DAF via bequest or through a planned giving instrument such as a charitable remainder trust or life insurance. You can name your children, grandchildren or others as the advisors to the DAF, establishing or furthering your family's tradition of giving. What a nice gift to leave for heirs!

A donor advised fund can be established at your local community foundation; with a financial institution or commercial sponsor that has a charitable gift fund (the best known are those managed by Vanguard, Fidelity, Charles Schwab, T. Rowe Price and other investment institutions); with an independent sponsor such as the National Philanthropic Trust or

American Endowment Foundation; or even at some charities themselves. Many small financial planning and investment firms now offer DAFs for their clients as well.

It is important to remember that once you have made a donation to a DAF, the donation belongs to the charitable fund itself. Technically, you as the original donor can only "recommend" the charities to which distributions should be made. Virtually all DAFs follow those recommendations closely as long as the beneficiary charities you have earmarked are legitimate 501(c)(3) exempt organizations.

Also, be aware that distributions from your donor advised fund cannot be used to fulfill the terms of a financial pledge you have made to a charity, nor can they be used to pay for charity event tickets or similar benefits.

4. **I've been reading about "socially responsible investing" and philanthropy – what is it?**

"Socially responsible investing" (or "SRI") refers to a process of aligning your financial investment decisions with your charitable giving goals. More specifically, it is the art and science of maximizing the social impact of your philanthropic investments through your personal investments.

An example can best illustrate the principle of SRI: it does not make much sense to support the local domestic violence shelter, on the one hand, while not knowing whether your portfolio or mutual fund might include stock in a liquor or weapons manufacturer on the other.

There are six levels of socially responsible investing that you and your family might want to explore:

LEVEL 1: Do no harm to the causes that matter to you most.

Screen your investment portfolio or mutual fund holdings to eliminate clear conflicts between your specific charitable passions and your stock investments, as in the example above.

LEVEL 2: Do no harm to the cause of mankind's general welfare.

Assess your holdings to determine whether any of the companies or funds are involved in products, services, or business practices that you feel are not in the general interest of society. Consider moving funds away from those firms.

LEVEL 3: Align your investing with companies whose values you respect.

Seek out investment opportunities where there are clear commonalities between your philanthropic passions and the services, products, and business practices of the companies in which you hold shares.

LEVEL 4: Invest in funds whose philanthropic goals closely match your own.

Actively invest in funds or companies whose philanthropic giving focuses on those same areas and interests as your own major gifts, in effect leveraging your contributions with your investments.

LEVEL 5: Use your power as a shareholder for the greater good.

Stay informed about shareholder resolutions under consideration at the companies whose stocks you hold, and vote your proxies in a manner consistent with your philanthropic values. When moved by your charitable values, do not be afraid to file and promote a shareholder resolution.

LEVEL 6: Invest in charity...literally.

Consider making direct loans or loans through an organizational intermediary in philanthropically-based projects. Such loans, or community development investments, can range from construction bridge loans for charities awaiting capital campaign pledge fulfillments, to investing in housing or a shopping center in a disadvantaged area, to purchasing and renting office space to nonprofits for less than fair market value.

Socially responsible investing is growing in popularity and many investment institutions, large and small, now offer funds that have been "screened" to filter out companies that an investor may wish to avoid for philanthropic reasons. By 2006, $2 trillion – or 13% – of professionally managed money in the U.S. was invested in screened or socially responsible funds. And you don't have to forego a healthy financial return if you engage in socially responsible investing. In just one example, the Domini 400 Social Index – the oldest index fund of socially screened companies – has earned returns virtually equal to the S&P 500.

If you are interested in program-related investments, speak with one of the larger community foundations or community loan funds in your area.

5. Our family has been talking about establishing a foundation – where do we start?

Start by speaking with your family's chief financial advisor: financial planner, investment counselor, estate or financial planning attorney, or senior accountant. It is important that your interest in establishing a foundation makes sense in terms of your family's overall financial goals and plans. Your professional advisor should be knowledgeable and experienced in charitable gift planning, charitable tax planning, and foundation fundamentals.

Once that advisor has helped develop a financial and administrative plan for your foundation, contact philanthropic counsel or a philanthropic advisor to work with you in defining your foundation's mission, goals, objectives, giving guidelines and practices, and due diligence systems.

The International Association of Advisors in Philanthropy is the professional association of financial planners and legal advisors with expertise in philanthropy and foundations. The Association for Small Foundations and The National Center for Family Philanthropy offer excellent resources geared toward the small or start-up foundation. The Council on Foundations is the largest support organization for organized private philanthropy.

Generally speaking, starting a private foundation is a wise option in terms of overhead costs and administrative requirements only if the foundation's initial assets will total several million dollars. For amounts less than that, a donor advised fund may be the better alternative.

6. A local charity looking to expand has asked us to consider funding a "feasibility study" – what is that?

A feasibility study is a structured research process for determining whether a planned building, program or service is needed, desired, and financially sustainable by the community it is intended to serve.

Most often, a charity will conduct a feasibility study in anticipation of a capital campaign to build a new facility or significantly expand an existing structure. Because such a project can cost millions of dollars, any prudent charity will start with a feasibility study to determine whether the community has the interest and financial means to support the project's high cost.

A feasibility study (or "marketing design study") conducted by an independent third-party firm specializing in capital campaigns will cost in the low five-figure range – a prohibitive expense for many charities. But a thorough study will result in both a definitive finding, and if the finding is positive, a detailed campaign plan that an organization must have before it commits to a massive and expensive project.

The axiom "penny wise, pound foolish" is central to the planning phase for a capital project. Your donation to support a feasibility study is an excellent philanthropic investment, whatever the study's outcome. Just be sure that the charity utilizes a reputable and experienced consultant or firm to conduct the study, and request that you receive a copy of the final study report.

7. If I'm making a substantial donation shouldn't I get a board seat?

Board seats should be reserved for only those individuals who have the highest level of passion for the charity's mission, a thorough understanding of a director's legal and fiduciary duties, and can make the commitment of time and attention necessary to the governance and oversight of a nonprofit corporation. In addition, prospective directors should have expertise and a temperament that complement those of the existing directors, and exhibit a willingness to contribute financially at a level commensurate with their means. If you possess those attributes, there is no reason for you to be excluded from consideration for a board position – in fact, you would be the ideal board candidate! But a large donation alone does not qualify one for a governance position.

If you have some concern about the use of your contribution, the financial accountability of the organization, or its investment policies, you might wish to volunteer to serve on the finance or audit committees on the board. Most board committees provide for non-director members.

8. How can I insure that our gift will remain anonymous?

The question is whether you want to remain anonymous to the organization or to the general public. If you wish not to have your gift publicized, be sure to speak to the Executive Director or the Vice-President or Director of Development about this before you make your gift. Explain that you do not wish to be acknowledged for this gift in any public manner, including the charity's newsletter or website. When making your gift, include those instructions in writing. If mailing or dropping off the gift, do so in a sealed enveloped addressed personally to the executive with whom you spoke. If transferring stock or other asset, be sure your representative in the transaction communicates those same instructions.

You will need to tell the organization how you wish the gift to be recorded in the charity's donor database, and whether they may use that information when contacting donors in the future.

Remaining totally anonymous – even to the charity itself – is a more difficult proposition, especially if you will require a written acknowledgement for tax purposes. You may be able to make your gift through an attorney or financial professional who will ensure that appropriate documentation is provided.

If you have a donor advised fund (DAF), you can recommend that a distribution be made to the charity, but instruct the fund manager to keep your identity confidential when making the gift. A receipt will not be necessary in this case, as you will have already received your charitable tax deduction at the time you funded your DAF.

9. **Two volunteer leaders from a local nonprofit came to our home recently and asked us to make a specific six-figure gift – how did they come up with that number?**

The charity could have arrived at that number through several different means. Perhaps a friend or associate who knows you well suggested to the charity that you might consider and could afford such a gift. Or the organization looked at other donations you have made to similar or local charities, and decided to solicit you for a comparably-sized contribution.

If you were interviewed during a "feasibility study" you were likely asked to give an indication of whether and to what extent you might consider financially supporting the project under discussion.

Most likely, however, when a gift of that size is requested, the charity engaged in some extensive homework before deciding on the figure. Many organizations – particularly larger ones such as colleges, hospitals, major museums and similar – employ what is known as a "prospect researcher." More and more smaller charities are contracting such professionals on an as-needed basis.

This prospect researcher's mission is to identify likely targets for major gifts, and to prepare a comprehensive and confidential financial and personal profile on each. Prospect researchers derive their information from an exhaustive array of public records.

A comprehensive profile may include information such as estimated total net worth; degree of liquidity; value of real estate, business and stock holdings; tax liability and lien information; business loan and mortgage information; court filing and civil actions; upublished address and telephone listings; luxury purchases; and even information about prenuptial or divorce agreements. Health status and other personal information that could be relevant might also be included. Equally important to the profile is information about other charities supported by the prospect, the range of amounts donated and for what; and any information about corporate or family foundations or trusts with which the prospect is associated.

The prospect researcher summarizes the findings in a report that includes a recommendation for the size of gift to be solicited. This profile report is then utilized by the chief development officer to design a specific strategy for engaging the prospect in a manner that could likely lead to that substantial a gift.

10. How do I handle all the requests from neighborhood children to buy wrapping paper, candy, cookie dough, magazine subscriptions and other items for their schools' fundraising campaigns?

If you want to be well-liked, buy a little something from everyone. However, if you want to be a wise donor, offer to make a donation to the school in the same amount you would have spent if you bought these items. When you buy wrapping paper and other products, the school receives only a small percentage of the purchase price. If you don't need the item being sold, write a check to the school directly so it can benefit from the entire amount.

Expect to be a little less liked, however, by the children. They are often competing for prizes for those who sell the most product. If this is the case in your neighborhood, call the school principal and suggest that children should also be acknowledged for contributions they collect.

11. A fellow community leader has called and asked for an appointment with myself and my wife to discuss plans for a new arts center building. We know this is not a project we will support. How and when do we tell him this?

Please let the caller know right away that due to other charitable commitments, you would not be in a position to consider a gift for the new arts center at this time. Do request they send you information on the project and promise to call them should you have any questions.

The unspoken rule among fundraisers is that when the prospect agrees to a visit, they already know they are going to be solicited. So, by agreeing to the visit, you are implying that you are at least open to considering a gift. If you know this is not something you would support, spare yourself and the caller the inconvenience of a pointless visit by politely declining.

12. I've been asked to serve on the board of a start-up charity – will I be expected to donate?

Ask yourself whether, as a donor, you would contribute to a charity whose own board members have not each made a donation. Your answer should be a resounding, "No!" By agreeing to serve on a board of directors, it is your ethical obligation to advance the mission of the organization through your time, talent, and financial treasure.

Others in the community will look to your example when considering their own contribution. And it will be far easier and more comfortable for you to solicit donations from others once you have made your own.

Every director should make an annual gift to the charity (a "gift" is an amount over and above the cost of attending fundraising events, purchasing raffle tickets, etc.). Some boards will be quite direct and specific about the size of contribution expected from its directors. When no dollar requirement is stated, a good rule of thumb is for each director, during his or her years of board service, to donate 80% of their annual charitable giving – excluding gifts to their faith organization – to the charity on whose board they serve.

For example, if you routinely donate a total of $1,000 to charity per year, $800 of that should be directed to the charity you govern during your years of board service. If your total annual giving is $100,000, $80,000 would be an appropriate amount to donate.

Some might think this is an extraordinary expectation. Service as a board director, however, implies an "extra-ordinary" level of passion and commitment to the mission, and a knowledge and faith in the operation such that this organization deserves a comparable philanthropic investment on your part.

13. We recently donated a large amount to a local shelter – weeks later, the charity's long-time executive director left her job. Shouldn't they have told us that when we made our gift?

Most charities will only announce the departure of their top executive if the person is retiring or moving out of the area by personal choice. If your confidence in the organization is based, in substantial part, on your faith in its top executive, have a frank discussion with the Board President, and separately with the Executive Director, prior to making your gift to determine whether changes at the top are anticipated. Unfortunately, the answers you receive may not be reliable. Consider breaking your donation into timed increments, or restricting the gift in such a way that a change in management would not affect the effective use of your gift.

14. If we decide not to donate to a particular charity because we've observed some weaknesses in the organization when performing our due diligence, should we tell the charity, and who would we tell?

Most charities would welcome candid feedback from prospective donors. You may have spotted some issues that were not apparent to the organization's leadership, and which may have deterred other donors as well. A brief letter stating your concerns should be sent to both the Board President and to the Executive Director. To be most helpful to the charity, focus on facts rather than on opinions. Offer to meet with one or both leaders privately to further discuss your concerns if it would be helpful to the organization. And explain how those issues would need to be addressed in order for you to reconsider a contribution.

15. What's the best way to handle an over-the-phone donation request?

Tell the caller that you will only consider requests made in writing. Do not get into a discussion over the phone about the charity or your giving interests, and NEVER provide credit card, social security number, age or other personal information to a telemarketer. Some will even agree to send you information, but will still press you to "suggest" what amount you may give. That's the time to end the call.

16. When hurricanes, terrorist attacks or other unexpected disasters occur, what's the best way to make a donation to help?

Rule number one when considering a disaster relief donation is "Wait!" It may be two weeks before enough information can be gathered to determine exactly what critical needs exist and which charities are best responding to the crisis. And many needs arising from a disaster may not even be known until some time after the event itself.

When Hurricane Katrina hit the U.S. Gulf coast, the world's attention was focused on the immediate needs of the survivors. Within one month, however, thousands of those survivors were relocated to far-away communities stretching from New England to California, where their needs included housing, food, clothing, work, and the supplies of daily living. Local charities in those communities were strained to the breaking point, trying to serve their existing client base as well as caring for the newly arrived. The value of your donation to a local charity at that time may have been much higher than a gift to a national organization in the immediate aftermath of the hurricane.

It is our instinctive response as caring people to want to help in the very moment of crisis. Wise and caring people will wait to see where critical, unmet needs require attention after the media has moved on to the next story.

17. **What does a philanthropic advisor or philanthropic counsel do, and when should I use one? Doesn't my financial advisor do the same thing?**

Philanthropic advisors specialize solely or primarily in assisting you or your family with discovering and defining your personal or philanthropic passion, and in guiding you in identifying organizations that meet those interests with respect to mission, size, location, maturity, financial need and risk. Most often they work side-by-side with your financial planner, estate planning advisor, or attorney

Philanthropic advisors are proficient in performing charitable due diligence and can recommend methods by which you can minimize the risk that your gift will be misused or underutilized. They can offer options for leveraging a gift – for example, SRI techniques – that can maximize your donation's positive impact on an organization.

A philanthropic advisor will often assist your financial or legal advisor in establishing your family foundation. They are proficient in helping you develop your foundation's mission, governance policies, giving guidelines and procedures, and strategic and long-range plans. They can also serve as very effective facilitators for family or foundation board retreats.

Some philanthropy consultants are themselves attorneys, financial planners, planned giving experts, or investment managers. The best philanthropic advisors, however, have "worked the other side," so to speak, during their professional career. That is, they have worked directly and extensively with charities as either an executive or a consultant. The strongest philanthropic advisors understand from experience what to look for when assessing a charity's true gift-worthiness, and are the professionals best qualified to recommend structuring the use or conditions of your charitable gift to maximize its philanthropic impact.

You or your financial or legal advisor would engage professional philanthropic counsel when you wish to deepen or expand your charitable activities, when you require that due diligence be performed on a charity, or when you are planning a family meeting around the topic of philanthropy and legacy. Absolutely bring in philanthropic counsel when the charitable component of your proposed estate plan involves gifts in the six-figure range and higher.

18. How do philanthropic advisors charge?

Philanthropic advisors may charge an hourly fee – rates will be comparable to those of an attorney – or they may quote a project fee based on the specific scope of work you or your financial planner or attorney have requested. Be wary of advisors who charge on the basis of your assets or on the donation amounts you are considering. Decide whether you would prefer that the philanthropic advisor contract directly with you, or whether you would prefer that they work under the umbrella of your financial or legal advisors.

It is imperative that your philanthropic counselor be committed to working collaboratively and cooperatively with your financial planner or attorney, and always in your best interest. You will want to confirm that the advisor does not and will not accept a commission, fee, or other material benefit from any charity they might evaluate or recommend; that they will disclose any existing or potential conflicts of interest; and that any and all of your personal and financial information is and will remain confidential.

19. What is the simplest and most efficient way to stay informed about new trends in philanthropy, different methods for giving, the latest thinking about the charitable sector, etc.?

Blogs related to philanthropy cover the most up-to-date thinking about the sector and about how to be a more active and effective donor. Some of the best blogs are written by top thinkers in the sector, as well as by very active donors and charity leaders.

AND THE MOST IMPORTANT QUESTION OF ALL...

20. YOUR question!

Do you have a question about charitable giving or philanthropy that you would like answered by an expert? Visit www.SmartGenerosity.com and click on MY FAQ.

EPILOGUE

"Has it occurred to anyone that a generation of generous giants is passing from our midst and when they've gone we may never see their like again?...

This was the generation that survived the worst depression in this nation's history, only to be plunged into the greatest war in the world's history, and then was battered by inflation only to emerge from it all stronger and more productive than ever before ...

This was a generation that grew up in hard times when jobs were scarce and salaries were low and higher education was for rich men's sons and credit was hard to get. Automobiles were a luxury few could afford, so this was a less mobile generation than the more affluent ones to follow. So whole families grew up and worked in well-defined neighborhoods, proud of their ethnicity and unashamed to express loyalty to government and respect for institutions.

This was a "nose to the grindstone" group of people who believed in the work ethic and "being a good neighbor" and a "day's work for a day's pay" and church every Sunday.

They were the men and women who built the nation's greatest institutions, businesses, industries and service organizations. They created the middle class in America and now, in the twilight of their years, those among them who enjoyed the greatest material success remain the financial backbone of thousands of non-profit hospitals and foundations and charities dedicated to the betterment of the health and welfare of all Americans. They are the funders, the donors, the endowers, and they have been exceedingly generous. But a chilling thought occurs.

When they've gone, who will take their place?"...

– Don Bresnahan
Documentarian & Film Writer

INDEX

SHARE
SMART GENEROSITY
WITH OTHERS!

Smart Generosity is available for
purchase at special quantity discounts:

- Premiums
- Client gifts
- Donor gifts
- Corporate gifts
- Sales promotions
- Fundraising

- Desk reference
- Trustee training
- Professional
  development programs
- Academic programs

Customized books or book excerpts can also be
created to fit your specific needs

For more information and to order, contact:
SpecialOrders@SmartGenerosity.com

or visit our website:
http://www.SmartGenerosity.com

More Valuable Resources

Learn more about practicing philanthropy, giving wisely, and making change in the world by visiting our home on the Web:

www.SmartGenerosity.com

There, you can find additional resources, information and learning opportunities, including:

- Our free online *Smart Generosity* e-newsletter
- On-demand teleseminars for donors, charities, and financial professionals
- Schedule of upcoming live events
- Special reports and white papers
- The Smart Generosity Blog

Smart Generosity Live!

Bring *Smart Generosity* to your family, clients, donors, foundation or conference with a customized keynote, presentation, workshop or retreat. For complete details on topics and fees, contact Events@SmartGenerosity.com

Special for Professionals …

For professional advisors, we offer confidential client consultations to assist you in offering the fullest range of philanthropic advisory services that discriminating clients have come to expect. We are also available for client appreciation events, special presentations for women of wealth, intimate philanthropy "salons," and in-house *Smart Generosity* training seminars.

Board retreats and family retreats are our specialty and are always customized to the specific needs of the client. We can offer facilitation for the full retreat, or participate in a special session only.

Coaching & Consulting ...

Renata Rafferty offers the *Smart Generosity* Donor Coaching program for individuals, families, and trustees of small foundations who would like personalized support in establishing and maintaining a clear focus in their philanthropic activities. Both coaching and consulting are available on a one-time, limited-term, or continuing basis. Small group coaching programs are also available.

A Final Request ...

To the many, many readers who have contacted me since the publication of *Don't Just Give It Away*, my deepest thanks. Your stories – and the stories of your clients and donors – were both inspiring and humbling.

My goal is to build a world-wide community of proactive, mindful philanthropists who focus and apply their financial resources – regardless of amount – toward making some specific positive change in the world that reflects their personal and family values and vision.

If this book has made a significant impact on how you think about charitable giving, or on your philanthropic activities, please know that I would love to hear about your success. Let me know how you – and the charities you support – are benefiting from engaging in *Smart Generosity*. And, if there is something you think I missed in this book, please send me your suggestions – you are my greatest inspiration.

Please e-mail me at Success@SmartGenerosity.com. I promise you that if you e-mail to us, I'll read it.

I look forward to hearing about your success!

⊷ ABOUT THE AUTHOR ⊷

Renata J. Rafferty is the author of the bestseller *Don't Just Give It Away: How To Make the Most of Your Charitable Giving*, and is regarded as the nation's leading donor advocate.

She has served as confidential advisor to some of the wealthiest families and institutions around the globe, and has assisted over one thousand charities, giving her an unparalleled perspective on the high-stakes world of charity and philanthropy.

Mrs. Rafferty has been interviewed by dozens of publications, including *INC.*, *Kiplinger's*, *Worth*, *On Wall Street*, *Research*, *Forbes*, *BusinessWeek*, and *The Chronicle of Philanthropy*, among many others, and is regularly sought for comment by major dailies such as The Washington Post, The New York Times, and The Wall Street Journal.

Her unique message and dynamic no-holds-barred style contribute to her reputation as a both a highly-respected and popular media guest. She has served as a charity analyst and provided on-air commentary for CNN, MSNBC, Fox News, Bloomberg and NPR, as well as for major radio and television stations across the country.

She is also a prolific writer, and has penned hundreds of columns, articles, and reports for outlets including Gannett, Worth.com, *Seasons in the Sun*, and *Giving*. She was the Founding Editor of *Nonprofit Consulting Review*.

More than an "outside" analyst, Mrs. Rafferty is highly respected within the charitable sector itself. She has taught or lectured on philanthropy and charitable sector issues at the top universities in America, and has addressed major conferences, roundtables and symposia on topics ranging from social change to personal philanthropy.

She has assisted institutional clients as diverse as The National Ballet of Canada, The Jewish Federation Council, Pepperdine

University, The Chicago Academy of Science, and La Alianza Hispana. She has also advised numerous government agencies including the U.S. Department of Labor and the California State Library system. And, she served as special counsel to both the Foreign Investment Agency and the Ministry of Foreign Economic Affairs for the Republic of Poland. In her work overseas, Mrs. Rafferty has advised foundations and charities in Eastern Europe, and served with the staff of the Vatican.

Mrs. Rafferty is recognized as one of the true pioneers in the field of philanthropic counsel. She serves on the Advisory Board of the National Philanthropic Trust and on the Governance Committee of the International Association of Advisors in Philanthropy. She has been honored with numerous public and private sector citations for her contributions to the field and practice of philanthropy.

As President of Rafferty Consulting Group Inc., Renata Rafferty helps generous individuals, families, foundations, and corporations, at all levels of giving, to achieve greater results in their philanthropic activities.

She also assists financial advisors, attorneys, wealth managers, family offices and allied professionals in expanding their practice offerings and client services to include all aspects of philanthropic counsel.

To find out more about Renata Rafferty, *Smart Generosity* programs and training, and Mrs. Rafferty's availability to coach, consult, or speak for your next event, visit her website at www.SmartGenerosity.com